WALKING THROUGH FIRE

How I Left a Narcissistic Relationship and Became a Shamanic Healer

To Jo

You are a Lovely Soul

Love [illegible]

J.J. Jenneson

First printing: 2022

ISBN-13: 978-0995684935

Published by Butterfly House Publishing

British Cataloguing Publication Data:
A catalogue record of this book is available from The British Library.

Dedication

I dedicate this book with love to my brother Christopher, who believed in me; to my dear friend Nick; and to my grandfather – I heard his shamanic call. To my mother, who will always have a place in my heart. To my spiritual guides, who I would like to thank for their unconditional love and healing. And to you, my dear reader, and the wonderful journey ahead of you.

Contents

Foreword

From a little house in the woods in the Vale of Health, North London, comes a warm greeting to you, dear reader. You are about to embark on a powerful journey. So, how is it that I ended up being asked to write a foreword for this book? Well, as the pandemic got underway in the spring of 2020, I could no longer practise in person, so I reached out to fellow creatives via Zoom in an attempt to offer creative options, solace, inspiration and support. This outreach was how I first came to know J.J.

She chose my online Artist's Way Next Level course for people who wanted to delve deeper into their use of creativity as a spiritual practice. These are classes I have shared for the last 25 years, in 4 countries. They are based solidly on Julia Cameron's work, *The Artist's Way*. J.J. attended my 12-week classes between Spring 2020 and Winter 2021. She came seeking revelations and reconnection with her inner child. As she listened to her inner child, I watched the story unfold. This book was being written while we watched in real-time. Each class supported her writing and self-discovery as the believing mirrors we are meant to be for one another. This book is a chronicle of her journey to freedom. I am delighted to have been able to watch her grow and develop into the powerful healer and advocate she is today.

Because of my diverse training and background in music therapy, sound therapy, psychodrama and performance, my classes tend to be out of the ordinary and fairly entertaining. J.J.'s talents, curiosity and determination shone brightly from the very first Zoom class. We explored together the importance of intentionality, regularity of practice, and depth of exploration. If we were doing a group meditation, exploring charitable practices, or just tending to relationships with those we loved, what really transformed us was making a commitment to creativity as a regular and living part of each day. I watched her do just this, in each class. Her totem from our first class together was an eagle. In this book, she goes into detail about power animals and how they assist in our growth and self-discovery. Plato said, "The life which is unexamined is not worth living." But I would add that: "The unlived life is not worth examining, either!" J.J.'s journey is a story that needs to be told. Her courageous living and examination of her life will benefit all who are dealing with domestic abuse.

My fondest hope is that this book will inspire and inform you. Parts of it may even challenge concepts you hold dear. If you are able to suspend your disbelief and doubt your doubts, you are in for a great adventure. You might just find yourself resonating with parts of her story that mirror your life experiences and challenge you to embrace change. The exercises she includes are a generous call to adventure, if you are ready. Amidst the distractions, duties of daily life and demanding confusions of current times, she reveals a journey of hope and renewal. Enjoy this read – and know that you too are free to live your life each day with gentleness, compassion and joy.

Andrea Lowry, MA CP MT
info@soundpractices.org

Preface

I decided to write this book because I wanted to give hope and strength to others, especially women who are going through challenging and difficult times. Whilst divorcing my husband I experienced a shamanic calling, which led to my spiritual awakening, and which I share in these pages. Some readers may not be women themselves but may know someone experiencing abuse. This book will help readers to gain some important insights into the red flags that signal abuse. I also want to introduce readers to shamanism from a personal and practical perspective. The reader will get a deeply honest account of what a spiritual awakening feels like.

Shamanism is a spiritual practice that involves a practitioner who interacts with the spirit world through altered states of consciousness. Shamanic journeying is a way of finding information, answers, healing and wisdom. This is done by travelling through a non-physical reality. This is achieved by going into a trance and accessing the spirit realm. A shaman is someone who can communicate and influence the world of good and bad spirits. They can go into altered states of consciousness during a ritual, and seek out knowledge from the past, present and future, or the unknown, by supernatural means. Shamanism is not tied to any religion or creed and predates Christianity.

In 2012, I had a vision that I would meet a group of people and learn about shamanism. I felt the call to have a soul retrieval whilst I was going through my divorce in 2016. This seemed crucial to my survival. I had asked my guide to find a shaman so I could go deeper into learning about shamanic practices. I had been attending a Reiki group and a therapist happened to tell me about a spiritual centre near to where I grew up. I found this synchronicity interesting. Later, I met Les Fuller, a shaman who facilitates Shamanic Crow tribe workshops. It was at this workshop that I went on a powerful shamanic journey where my helping spirits gave me the title for this book. This is how *Walking Through Fire* was born.

This book is a personal and heartfelt memoir of how I got out of a narcissistic marriage and was able to go deeper within.

Shamanism is a deep spiritual practice. I give a brief introduction to shamanism and look at the historical aspects of how humanity was separated from our authentic self, and nature. A vampiric spirit is a type of mind virus that Native

Americans call 'Wetiko', and narcissism is looked at from a spiritual perspective. The reader will get insight into my own challenges and childhood trauma and how they impacted me as an adult.

There is stigma and shame around domestic abuse, and I wanted to shine a light on these issues to help people feel less alone. I wanted to bring these issues out of the darkness. Shamanism is about going within and seeing into the dark to find our own truths and uncover the illusions. It is in this way that we can wake up and remember who we truly are as spiritual beings. Shamanism allowed me to go within and find my personal power and freedom; it gave me the power to traverse a dark period in my life, ultimately finding light and relief on the other side.

The reader will learn about trauma from a shamanic viewpoint, and I will explain how soul and power loss occurred within my childhood. You will read a personal account of my own soul retrieval and I will talk about how to do shadow work, and how this played out in my marriage on an unconscious level. Leaving a narcissistic marriage felt like jumping off a cliff without a parachute. I had to deprogramme myself from fear and find the courage to begin the healing process.

Walking Through Fire is about being in the fire and not getting burnt. One of the themes is transformation. I also had to peel back the layers of fear around leaving a toxic situation and writing my truth. When one person writes their truth, it gives other people the courage to recognise their own truth. Part of my healing is about releasing the shame of marrying a narcissist and handing over my power. This book is about facing your shadows and going into the fire; it's about feeling the fire burn around you and knowing it will make you stronger.

Growth is uncomfortable, just like a seed that has to be in darkness before it can sprout, grow and bloom. Shamanic journeying was another tool I used to discover how to heal and find information about myself, and I give an in-depth example from the world of film. *The Wizard of Oz*, for example, has many shamanic themes around illusion and finding your courage. The reader will learn about power animals as a healing modality.

I also had an inner knowing that I am a first wave Indigo Adult. I had been researching the work of Delores Cannon since 2005 and had become interested in this subject. The universe was determined that I take notice and I would continue to come across articles and books and would find myself nodding my head in recognition. The book that changed my life is *Indigo Adults*, by Kabir Jaffe and Ritama Davidson.

We are highly sensitive and empathic souls who have been incarnated on earth to have the chance to fulfil our soul's life mission. It is my belief that our memories were erased when we incarnated on earth, and awakening activates us in order to remember who we are.

I had an interesting experience whilst writing my book. I was talking to my friend Lucy on a video call and I informed her that I was a warrioress in another lifetime, as I was always metaphorically fighting battles, and in a previous life I had died with a wound to my head. Suddenly the room filled with white healing light and from the right-hand side, near my eye, I saw a white arrow of light coming towards my head. I moved back and the arrow missed me. My friend saw this, and was in awe, and I laughed because I've always had an affinity with various warriors. For example, I have always loved *Star Wars*, especially when I found out the Jedi Order in the film are guardians of peace and justice. The Jedi Knights are warrior monks.

This really resonated with me and yes, it occurred to me that my intuition was spot on. I am indeed a brave warrior, especially with my words. I have had several guided meditations from my higher self from various past life experiences where I was a warrior in different timelines.

It felt like another level of my awakening to finally accept that I'm an Indigo soul; it felt ironic, because I felt truly awakened at the time of writing this book, yet everyone was in lockdown. Just as most people's power and freedom was taken away, I finally discovered my own. I believe the world is undergoing a mass awakening in terms of consciousness, in that people are questioning governments and how we are living our lives. People want an alternative education system, health and financial systems. I believe these systems will eventually break down so that a better world can be rebuilt. Many Indigos are waking up to their purpose.

This is the perfect time for Indigos, as our unique souls have come to assist humanity in the 'Great Awakening'.

This book looks at the manipulation programming that I endured within my marriage and how I broke free to rediscover my true power. It is the same fear programming that has been running the world for world for thousands of years. It is time for everyone to wake up and break free.

It is also about how I reconnected with and healed my inner child through *The Artist's Way* by Julia Cameron and by meeting wonderful helpers on my journey.

The biggest challenge with writing this book is that it's an unconventional memoir. I have included practical exercises, a history of shamanism and my own personal beliefs, all of which are interconnected throughout. I hope readers will find this three-in-one approach useful, although I certainly made it harder for myself. My intention is that this book provides a deeper look into a personal, unique transformation and spiritual awakening.

Awakenings

'She has been feeling it for a while now, that sense of awakening. There is a gentle rage simmering inside her, and it's getting stronger by the day. She will hold it close to her. She will nurture it and let it grow. She won't let anyone take it away from her. It is her rocket fuel and finally she is going places. She can feel it down to her very core – this is her time. She will not only climb mountains. She will move them too.'

Lang Leav

Chapter One: Freedom Papers

'You are free, da, da, da, da, like a bird in the sky, you can fly high in your mind, in your body, in your soul. I am free, I am free, I am free, I am freeeee, da, da, da, da.'

Freedom Song by J.J. Jenneson

Today was the day I had been dreading, but now it had actually come, it was a relief. It was the summer of 2018 and I was officially divorced. There was slight trepidation as I looked at the brown envelope. Ah – that must be what my solicitor had tried to warn me about. Nothing can really prepare you for how you will actually feel. As I held my decree absolute in my hand, I knew I had won my freedom. It felt like an anti-climax. The energy, heartbreak and struggle to get to this point, whilst living with my soon to be ex-husband, was not to be underestimated. How the hell did I do that?

I hate to admit it, but I was a coward. It took me seven years to pluck up the courage to start the process of divorce in order to end the subjugation I had endured for so many years. Looking back, I can see why it took me such a long time. But there is energy in numbers, and seven is my lucky number. Seven years marked its own kind of journey. It takes seven years for all the cells in your body to be regenerated and replaced.

Years ago, someone posed the question: "How would you feel being married to your husband for the next ten or twenty years?" I ruminated on that thought for five seconds. It was horrifying. My soul withered and died. How could I betray my soul like that? Would I even be able to look at myself in the mirror with any respect? That question would be at the back of my mind for years to come as I made the slow and painful decision to end my marriage. I was full of fear; I didn't think I could do it. I still had to learn how to become a warrior and fight for my life whilst under a quasi-dictatorship.

So, I was compelled to rediscover my bravery. I had imagined this day for a long time and often played the song *I Get Out* by Lauryn Hill. That song became my anthem as I vowed that I would never give my power away. The ex-husband hated the song. But when we lived under the same roof, I just played it louder, as a reminder of how I felt as I imagined a new life for myself.

I stared at the decree absolute for what seemed like an eternity. It took a while for it to sink in properly; eventually, it made everything real on a psychological level. I wondered how many other women were going through the same thing. It was like when I was pregnant and would see other pregnant women and give them that knowing look. I received that knowing look from other divorced women as well. I sat in the house contemplating what my new life was going to look like. But meanwhile, I had a more pressing issue.

I had found out that the gas boiler had a leak, and the offending leak was dripping through the concrete flooring. It was bad timing as I had my children with me for part of the summer holidays. I now realise we were lucky to be alive. The plumber said the leak was dangerous and if I hadn't called him at that very moment, the house would have literally blown up. In a way, the boiler was a reflection of my toxic marriage: a pressure cooker waiting to explode. Oh yes, and the repairs were going to cost me around £450 that I did not have. Actually, the plumber wanted to charge over £500 but agreed to a lower price.

The next challenge was to try to get the ex-husband to pay half. Technically, the house was his responsibility; I was now merely an occupant, as my name had never been on the mortgage or the deeds. It had become clear that he did this as another way he could be in control. The dysfunctional dynamics within the marriage had played out in the divorce process. The issue of money had always been a flashpoint within the marriage, and it wasn't going to go away. I tried to stand up for myself, but it was futile. I was literally worn down and stonewalled whenever I gave my opinion about the family home or financial affairs. I had the slow realisation that I had never been respected within the marriage. I had no voice, power or rights. I was screaming with sadness, but no one could hear me. I felt as if I was in captivity – but with the decree, now I was finally free.

But the path to freedom was costly, and not just the money for the boiler. I was now lumbered with extra bills, and I had to figure out a way of finding the money because my now ex-husband refused to pay half. Did I mention that the phone line had been cut off? Even the Sky channels had been cancelled without my knowledge.

The boiler leak was bad enough that we needed to turn off the gas for health and safety reasons. It turned out that the gas was supplied by EDF, the electricity company, and to complicate matters even more, the account was under the ex-husband's name; I couldn't get it put into my name, and they wouldn't take my calls because of data protection. According to EDF, I didn't exist as my name wasn't on the account. The person from the utilities company said, "Tell your husband he has to contact us." I phoned my ex-husband, but he refused. I phoned the company again. "Tell your husband it's an emergency and he has to." I did as I was told, but again he refused. I pleaded with my ex-mother-in-law, but she didn't want to get involved. The frustration was infuriating.

Anyway, on the fourth – or was it the fifth or sixth? – phone call, the ex-husband realised that in order for him not to appear totally heartless, he would have to contact the utility company after all. He tried to make out he was a hero and offered to have the kids, but no – he wasn't in charge anymore. I just wanted him to phone EDF and take his name off the account.

The kids thought it was hilarious, and complained that there was no internet, no TV, no gas and, to top it off, it had started raining – in August! Their only consolation was when I said: "Okay, we have no TV and no internet, but don't worry, because we are going to have takeaway for the next few days. Yay!" To the kids, I tried to make out like this was just a fun adventure that we would laugh about this time next year.

The ex-husband refused to pay any money for the boiler, and I was livid. As my friend Nick said, "It's one thing letting you suffer. But what about your kids? He's, their father. Why wouldn't he offer to pay half?" I would have paid him back, and I even put this in writing with a solicitor in case he thought I wouldn't. After all, my ex-husband was an accountant and he accounts for every penny. I would have kept my word. But eventually, I accepted that he wasn't going to pay anything.

Two days later, copper piping was put in via the boiler, and I'd sorted out a new phone line and set up a new TV package. I had all the bills in my name now, and the relief of not needing to ask for anyone's permission was like liberation. Bloody hell, I did good all by myself.

It was like when I still lived with my husband and I needed to have my mobile phone put in my name. He refused, citing that I couldn't have the house in my name either. I was humiliated when he spoke to the mobile phone company and point-blank refused. The woman at the company apologised profusely. However, I managed to convince him that I would pay my own phone bill. I pleaded my case and he relented after a few months. It was all about cost and benefits and I won my freedom to have the phone put into my own name at last. It felt like a small victory towards my agency. Back then, between 2012 and 2016, everything was so different.

I had no income of my own because I wasn't working yet, but I did have a laptop that belonged to me, and I was good at researching. While surfing the internet I came across a life coach named Lindsey Ellison. She offered a course called 'Divorcing a Narcissist'. I was intrigued and, late at night, I would listen to her live podcasts. I devoured every one of her articles on *Huffington Post*. I was becoming aware that I had to get out of my marriage. I had that horrible lightbulb moment of waking up to my reality and what I was up against.

"If only I could take her course," I would say to myself. At that time, I believed that the universe would help me to find a way, even if I could not see it yet. I decided to take drastic action and sell my wedding ring. I had stopped wearing it as a sign to myself that I was a free woman in my own right, and I belonged to myself. I sold the ring on Valentine's Day, of all days. Even I could see the irony in my defiant act. Unfortunately, I was five pounds short for the course but, as I was walking back towards our house, I saw a five-pound note in the middle of the pavement. It was right in front of me! Well, that felt like an act of love sent from the universe, and it was a good enough reason to do the course. My work with Lindsey Ellison was just the beginning, as I realised I wanted to create many other changes in my life, too.

I was looking for deeper meaning within my life and I found it as I rediscovered my creative soul through reading *The Artist's Way*, by Julia Cameron. The book is about how creativity leads you on a spiritual path through rediscovering your own creativity. I was absolutely sold on the idea because I wanted to shift my consciousness to a higher level. Cameron advocates going for walks, journaling and taking time to have play dates by yourself.

I found a group for the twelve-week Artist's Way course but the day didn't work for my husband, as he played football on a Thursday, and he wasn't going to give that up for me. I needed a miracle of some kind, but how was that going to happen? The course was due to start in a week, and just before it started, my husband came home to say that he had injured his toe whilst playing football. I found out it would take approximately twelve weeks to heal properly. This gave me the perfect opportunity to find some freedom, one step at a time.

Chapter Two:
How Did I Get Here?

'In order to heal properly you must walk away from what broke you.'

RH Sin

I had to step back into the past and reflect on events from my childhood to find out why and how I ended up in this marriage. I began to reflect on my own trauma and what had happened in my marriage, and the ex-husband's parents' marriage, and my ex-husband's family. Shamanism is a good modality for healing any type of trauma.

Soul loss has to do with someone losing a part of their soul or essence through an event such as the death of a loved one, accident, abuse, natural disaster or any other traumatic experience where the soul becomes fragmented. A part of the soul leaves the body to help the person deal with what is happening at that precise moment in time. Spirit is sent away to a 'safe place' until the danger passes. A person may lose their memory, for example, if they are in a dramatic car accident. This can also happen with emotional and sexual abuse.

Power loss occurs when we are disconnected from our true nature and our innate power. Typical symptoms of power loss are depression and chronic illness. Chronic misfortune occurs when we don't tap into our life force. Use of a power animal is one way to be able to create protection once more. When our energy feels diminished, this creates an opening in the body for other entities or viruses to enter the space. The universe does not like empty spaces; that is why it is good to have a power animal or spiritual guardian for protection. A shamanic practitioner can assist with finding the right power animal or guardian spirit to restore lost power and provide protection.

Thought forms are to do with how we think, and they can affect our emotions; unexpressed feelings create blockages within the body. Spiritual intrusions come from negative thought forms; indigenous cultures make the distinction between sending energy and expressing energy. That is why it's important to express negative emotions like frustration, anger and sadness. If we do not deal with these emotions, they become internalised within the body and create dis-ease and illness. When our mind and body is healthy, we are less likely to be affected by illness. From a shamanic viewpoint, energy never dies; instead, it is transmuted or transformed.

I lost my mother when I was nine years old, and she too had suffered trauma as her mother died before I was born. I don't think I was able to process her death at all. Back then in the eighties, people were just expected to get on with things and there was not much help for children dealing with loss. I didn't think it had affected me greatly; however, I went to see a reiki healer while I was pregnant and she said that I was grieving. I was stunned because my mother had died such a long time ago. How could I be still be grieving? To me, it didn't make sense. However, from a shamanic point of view, any type of trauma can be a source of soul loss, and time is not linear.

There are many common symptoms of soul loss. One of the most common ones is dissociation, where a person does not feel fully in his or her body or fully engaged in life. Other symptoms include depression and unending grief that just does not heal. Maybe the fact that I didn't think about it on a subconscious level was the issue. Little was I to know that if trauma is not treated or acknowledged properly it leaves energetic holes in the body that allow for spiritual pain. The way this manifests is by not having strong personal boundaries and it creates an opportunity for abusive people or situations to enter our lives. Hence, I met my husband and a cycle of abuse continued horrendously over a number of years. Once I realised the effect it was having on me, I knew I had to leave.

What I didn't realise was that my mother's death was going to change my life in so many profound ways. I was challenged to step into my true power. Instead, I married someone I thought would be a life partner who turned out to have strong narcissist traits. I would continue on my path of self-discovery experiencing something negative, but that would ultimately lead to my own spiritual awakening on all levels. It was going to force me to face my wounds so that I would become what is known as a 'wounded healer'. It was part of my soul's journey to have this traumatic experience so I could become a spiritual alchemist and be able to help others.

My ex-husband's family had suffered their own trauma from deaths and mental illness. I can now see how the things that happened to my ex-husband's father left invisible scars. It also created certain belief systems around the treatment of women within the family. There was one incident that will be etched in my memory forever. I could have learned a lot by watching how he treated his wife. We were in the car, visiting wedding venues in Eastbourne, and my soon-to-be mother-in-law was giving directions. The father-in-law started getting annoyed and then he went into a terrible rage at his wife. He was really angry and calling her horrible names. I just sat there thinking that my future husband wouldn't ever talk to me like that – until he did.

My now ex-husband had bought a wardrobe and needed help to assemble it. I was always accommodating towards him and agreed to help him. The wardrobe was huge, and it was difficult to hold in place while the husband attempted to put it up. The wood kept slipping out of my hand, and it was really frustrating. And then he began to berate me and started swearing at me, just like I had seen his father do in the car all those years ago. I realised very clearly that he was using exactly the same words his father had back then. Unlike his mother, who said nothing and pretended it wasn't happening, I decided I wasn't going to put up with this; I was not going to smile and act like this was normal behaviour. Oh no, I wasn't going to take it – so I said, "You know what? I'm not helping you anymore," and I just walked away in disbelief.

In the early days of my marriage, I would talk to and confide in his mother. I was really surprised when she said her husband would give her the silent treatment and not talk to her for days. She said at first it had bothered her but now she didn't care. She had clearly decided to put up with it and her solution was to be nice. Her husband would put her down in subtle ways by inferring that she wasn't intelligent. Their daughter (my ex-sister-in-law) would be visibly upset and call out her father for being unkind. Meanwhile, my then-husband and father-in-law would not say anything. My mother-in-law would smile at her daughter to thank her for sticking up for her, but she did not ever stand up for herself. I saw this dysfunctional behaviour plays out for many years. I can only imagine what the children had witnessed in their formative years.

Sometimes my ex-sister-in-law would put on a baby voice and

while I found it amusing at times, I now see it as a poor coping mechanism. I noticed this would happen at Christmas time, and only when she was around her parents. I found it strange for a grown woman to behave this way. I have since read that some psychologists say women do this if there has been some kind of trauma before the age of puberty. No one really knows what type of childhood other people experience. Maybe this was her way of dealing with the uncomfortable ways the family related to each other. I could see the frustration she had with the way her father treated her mother.

Meanwhile, her brother would often sugar-coat his childhood as being perfect and happy. He told me his dad lost his own father quite young and was critical about him, although he did have a stepfather. I could read between the lines. I knew my ex-husband's father was strict and his mother over-compensated and praised her son because she felt that was the best thing she could do under the circumstances. His father told him that if he did not do well at school, he would end up working as a binman. I shook my head when I heard that because it was said from a place of fear. I can only guess he said that to motivate his children to work hard at school. What I feel is that their childhood wasn't as perfect as the picture my ex-husband was trying to paint. I can see that he was affected by his father's treatment of his mother and that this could be why he treated women in a certain way throughout his adulthood. What we need to get clear on is that our childhood experiences affect our adult lives. On the outside looking in, I could see clearly that they were dysfunctional to a certain degree – and this played out cruelly as I started the divorce process.

Over the years, the silent treatment had become a common occurrence within my own marriage. On occasion, I would ask my husband what I had done, but all I heard was silence. I had endured this dysfunctional behaviour for years. I realised this was his way of treating me if I disagreed with him or gave my opinion. I learnt to shut down emotionally. If I asked my husband another question, he would ignore me for days, which turned into weeks, months and then years once the marriage was falling apart. That behaviour was damaging not only to myself but also to our children because they picked up on what was going on energetically, even when I acted as if it didn't matter. He would talk to the kids and ignore what I said. I tried to paper over the cracks and create some type of normalcy for our children. So, I would just talk to the kids. It wasn't that obvious because I was with the kids during the day, and they were happy to see their dad in the late evening.

It was quite clear that he didn't want to be in my company. It got to the point where we would go to bed at different times. I was beyond miserable. I thought this was what I deserved. This is how low my self-esteem was at the time. I wasn't allowed to sit in the front of the car and was relegated to the back, like a child. He made sure our kids laughed at me and I was the butt of jokes as well, in the same way his father ridiculed his mother. I knew then that I had to get out of the marriage – but first I needed information. I needed a plan, because I knew there was something not quite right with my husband. I'd realised he was a narcissist and I had to find a safe way out. He wanted total power and control, especially around money.

Chapter Three: It's All About the Money

'A narcissist never "steals" money because in his mind, it's all his.'

Unknown

A narcissist loves power and uses money to control and dominate. Being a typical empath, I primarily want to feel secure. For me, dealing with money is a complex process going all the way back to when my mother died. I knew the adults around me at the time were anxious about this issue as there were three young children to take care of. As an empath, I absorbed that anxiety as I heard arguments about money. My sense of security was fractured, as was my relationship with money.

When my husband trained to become an accountant, he uses

this to take advantage of me economically. He had a strange 'black box' attitude to money. He didn't like to share it, even though we were married. Later, it became obvious that I had missed or ignored many red flags right back to when we first met.

A few weeks before I was going to be married, the priest came around to our flat in Hastings. We needed to discuss our vows and he wanted to include a verse about sharing our worldly goods. My fiancé was absolutely against this idea. "Oh, you don't like sharing," the priest said. My so-called husband-to-be was clearly offended and visibly angry with our canon, who was called Keith Pound (oh, the irony).

Keith was a jovial person, and really lovely. On his face was a look of 'Oh dear, this is not a good start to married life.' At the time, I just thought he was being cautious but in hindsight, this was a major red flag for all the right reasons. But I tried to put it to the back of my mind – although I was silently wondering why my husband would not want to share what he had, as was customary. To my mind, I wasn't materialistic, and I would be happy sharing with someone for our mutual 'worldly good'.

As my intuition was kicked in, I thought, "This man, who I am married to, is being too careful with his money," and, in my wiser moments, "If this doesn't work out, I can get out." Isn't hindsight a wonderful thing?

A couple of days before the wedding I was having doubts again because he wanted to micro manage the last-minute details of the wedding. He sensed my doubt and apologised for his behaviour. It seemed plausible at the time. However, it was a sign that the marriage was going to be built on sand. Once we were on our honeymoon, I knew I had made a terrible mistake, but I didn't want to think about it so I pushed the thought to the back of my mind. I had my 'back-up' plan that I could get divorced if things didn't work out in the future.

My financial situation quickly changed as, when we returned from the honeymoon, I found out I was pregnant. It felt like a miracle as I had been told by a doctor that I was infertile because of a medical condition I'd had since the age of twenty. We'd asked the canon who married us for a blessing for us to have children. "My blessings don't normally work that quickly!" he said when we told him. He was delighted for us. For practical reasons, I gave up my job as it would have been difficult to commute from Hastings to London. At the time, my husband had a mortgage in his name only and he refused to put the house in my name or to have his wage go into a joint account. Instead, he decided that a separate joint account would be kept.

When I first met him, he had come to London for a fresh start after running away from debts he'd accumulated when he lived in the north of England. I found it strange that he had a business account because he had no business to speak of. He did have some kind of consultancy, but it was all very strange. He was keen to move in with me and when he heard I had a clean credit history he thought it would be a good idea to get the electricity bill in his name but at my address. When we got married, he decided to put me on an allowance of £200 per month. He paid for all the bills, as he was working full-time and I had decided to take a two-year break from work while I was pregnant and with our child.

The issue of money was to come up in our marriage eleven years later. We were having marriage counselling and the counsellor asked my husband how he would feel if the roles were reversed and he was financially independent but gave up his job and was given an allowance by his wife. "Degraded," is what my husband said. The counsellor realised that my husband was a control freak. Again, as with the priest, he was getting angry with the counsellor for putting him on the spot – and he was caught out because of her observations.

It had taken me ten years to get him to go to counselling and I had just about given up. Having sensed that I didn't want to be with him anymore, and in a last-ditch attempt, he suggested counselling. He had phoned me up and was actually laughing. "Well, you have been asking me for ten years so we might as well give it a go." I agreed to go because by this time I had worked out that he was a narcissist and I still had to play the long game to get out of the marriage. By now I had a clear picture of what I was up against and I was working out a plan. He had an interest-only mortgage and lots of credit card debt that still had to be dealt with. But all I wanted was to be out of this nightmare situation. I knew he wasn't going to leave the marriage quietly. He had kept me in the dark for years regarding the family finances and had seemingly prepared himself well.

It is always easier to control someone with fewer resources and that is why women who are abused don't leave. If you have children, it is like a double bind because of the ineffective, painfully secretive and broken family court system, which is not educated about personality disorders, emotional or economic abuse, or parental alienation. Everything is stacked against the women because of the entrenched patriarchal system we still live under. Power and control in the form of money have been in the hands of men for thousands of years.

Economic abuse: behaviour that controls a person's ability to acquire, use or maintain economic resources, thus threatening their economic security and potential for self-sufficiency. - Definition of economic abuse by Adams et al, 2008.

At this point, I became acutely aware that my children were watching their own mother having to ask for money. I was seen as less equal in my children's eyes and that feeling didn't sit well with me energetically. My husband would complain about how he had no new clothing when he was a child, and had no problem spending hundreds of pounds on a new suit for work – and yet I was put on an allowance. Of course, I would say I thought this was wrong, but he would shut me down time and time again. It was obvious he wasn't going to change. Even when the marriage counsellor brought up the issue of the small allowance, he continued with his regime. He never intended to change this, although I made it abundantly clear I disagreed with it. It made me feel sad that our children had to see such a distorted view of money within a marriage at such a young age. My children believed that it was his money and house, when in fact it should have been a partnership.

The irony is that because I was good at paying all my utilities, that was what enabled my ex-husband to get a mortgage in the first place. He had used me to get a mortgage and then put it in his name only. There was a difference between the deeds and the mortgage application and he could have put my name on the deeds; I had spoken to a friend who hadn't worked for a very long time and her husband had put her name on the deeds.

He even said it was all about the money. It made me feel sick to hear this because it proved there was never any real love for me. He only really cared about the money and restoring his credit rating.

Chapter Four: Rose-Coloured Glasses

'As we gain confidence in ourselves, red flags are no longer red flags. They are deal breakers.'

Unknown

Upon reflection, I was to discover even more ways my husband had become strange around money. When I first met him, he was very generous and would pay for dinner, and I made the mistake of thinking that he was caring, when really this was a cover for his manipulation. Narcissists use money as a tool to manipulate feelings, especially in an intimate relationship. Really what I needed to do was to pay attention but unfortunately, I failed to do this. Rightly or wrongly, who doesn't appreciate someone who takes away all the little worrisome details of money?

I had been financially independent from a young age, as I left home when I was eighteen. Ironically, my saving grace was that I had always taken an interest in money and finance. My dad came from a well-to-do family as his parents had their own business in Nigeria. He had trained with the Royal Air Force and was a qualified bookkeeper. My mother was a nurse and came from a farming background in Jamaica. However, when my mother died, my sense of security was dashed. So, when I met this man who seemed confident and was ambitious, I thought I had made a good choice. Or did I? Of course, I did not know then that he had narcissist characteristics. Maybe there was a part of me that believed the marriage would give me a sense of security that I was lacking within myself, and life would be better with someone who had my back. I really wanted to believe we could build a secure future together.

When we dated in 2000, my husband was the kind of person who was happy to pick up the bill, and that was a classic way of showing what a great guy he was. However, narcissists only do this to get positive attention. A classic dynamic of domestic violence is the control of money. The one who has more money can take ownership of the person who has fewer resources, and the narcissist will regulate how and when the money is spent. Money became a dark space for me in the marriage as he had done such a good job of love bombing me during the dating process.

A warning to others: it is so easy to be swept up in the

moment... but what we actually need to be doing is paying attention to everything. What started as a fairy tale turned into a horror show once divorce was on the horizon. The face they show during divorce is not a mask but the true self they have been all along.

Suddenly the generosity disappeared. What was so traumatic for me was the realisation that he was absolutely controlling and anal about every minute detail of life. Suddenly he was pretending that he was a pauper, on a high salary but with debts. I spoke to a solicitor who confirmed that these tactics are common because in a marriage your partner's debt becomes your debt. My father had died in 2017 and my husband was trying to find out if there was an inheritance. I was not privy to a will, but divorcing spouses will try to get hold of any inheritance. Narcissists are extremely greedy as this is part of their sense of entitlement and grandiosity. This showed up again when he informed me not to get legal advice, that he had a financial plan in place and all I needed to do was sign it. I smelt a rat right away. The terms and conditions had so many clauses and subclauses, yet he encouraged me to sign it within twenty-four hours. Oh no – luckily, I wasn't going to fall for that.

The following are some of the traits of Narcissistic Personality Disorder, according to the Diagnostic and Statistical Manual of mental health:

- Behaving in an arrogant or haughty manner
- Exhibiting a sense of entitlement
- Exaggerated sense of self-importance
- Having an inability or unwillingness to recognise the needs or feelings of others
- Expecting unquestioning compliance with their expectations
- Taking advantage of others to get what they want

There are several red flags that indicate a possible narcissist, such as:

Love bombing: This is a tool that narcissists use to manipulate their targets. They do this by declaring love early on in the relationship, buying gifts and paying for extravagant dates. Love bombing is actually a form of grooming to lull their victim into a false sense of security.

A perfect match: A narcissist will make their target or victim feel as if they are the perfect partner. This is done at the beginning of a relationship to get the target to fall for them.

Speedy does it: They move quickly to secure their target by making the relationship exclusive and spending a lot of time together. This is done so the other person does not have time to analyse or evaluate what is happening.

Who's who: The narcissist will ask lots of questions. Of course, it is normal to ask questions to gauge whether a person is worth your time and attention, especially when you are dating. However, the narcissist tries to get as much information as they can to assess how easy it will be to override your personal boundaries and manipulate you further down the line.

Hide and seek: They will hold onto any personal disclosure for negative reasons and will eventually use it to devalue and disregard you. Everything you say to them will be used as a reference point to steal from you and manipulate you. Narcissists have no qualms about lying because it comes naturally to them; they have been lying for most of their lives. In a healthy relationship, vulnerability is not used against you, and is an accepted part of an individual; the narcissist will use it against you, especially if you try to leave them. They view you leaving them as abandonment and this taps into their own unresolved wounds from their childhood. Remember, they abandoned their spiritual core essence long ago.

Using charm: this goes from charm to harm over a long period of time. Narcissists have good presentation skills at the beginning of a relationship, which they use as a mask. But it is not a sustainable act.

Centre of the world: Moving the relationship into an intense phase by phoning and texting all the time can happen quickly.

An example of this would be to move in quickly and say they are in love or that you are their soulmate: "No one understands me like you do." This is done to hook the target. It triggers a need in many people to find fairy-tale solutions, especially if they grew up in co-dependent families.

Sadly, sociopaths and narcissistic personality disorders go together like peas and carrots. The traits of a sociopath, known medically as Anti-social Personality Disorder, include:

- Driven by a need to increase their self-esteem through personal gain and power
- Pleasure is often at the expense of others
- Having little or no concern for the feelings, needs or suffering of others
- Lack of remorse after mistreating another person
- Unable to have healthy mature relationships
- Uses dominance, intimidation to control others
- Manipulates others for their own gain
- Cold and calculating to other people
- Uses charm and can act sincere
- Hostile, irresponsible and impulsive

- Exploitive, deceitful and use coercion

Here are some of the signs of a sociopath.

So wonderful: They are very charming and friendly in a superficial way. They normally want something, such as sex, money or shelter. They can turn the charm on and off at a whim as long as the ends justify the means.

What a great person: They seem to be too good to be true. A sociopath will love the things you love; for example, they will have very similar musical tastes to you. Sociopaths can even fool the FBI. I was watching a crime programme and a man who was high up in the organisation was interviewing a candidate, who they accepted. Yet he realised early on that the man would bring the organisation down. "If only I had listened to my gut," he said. "The truth of the matter is that he was too perfect." If something seems too good to be true – it usually is.

One-stop shopping: The sociopath will find out what your needs and wants are and will make sure they can fulfil those needs. They systematically make a mental note of these and file them away for use at a later date.

Pinocchio syndrome: They lie compulsively to benefit and uplift themselves, but it is hard to believe they can lie like that in the early phase of the relationship.

Be my saviour: Sociopaths have addictive personalities and are emotionally unstable. “You are the only one who can help me.” This is why they go into rage attacks if they are criticised.

Control: This is their game. They need to know when, how and why something will be done. It must also always be done their way.

Chapter Five: A Mother's Wound Parental Alienation

'The truth hurts; that's why so many ignore it.'

Marie Forleo

The divorce was really a new beginning, and I had to feel the grief and other emotions that came with that experience. Julia Cameron talks about anger and how people are afraid of it. She says to use it instead as fuel. The anger I felt showed me how I had been mistreated. I realised I could use my experience to help others, and there was a higher purpose for all that I had experienced. I began to listen to my higher self and make a new life. For the first time I could clearly see manipulation, greed, control and fear in the world and how it impacted people's lives. My higher self gave me clear instructions, and this time I was going to listen. I was to trust myself and my guides. This advice felt serious, and I noticed subtle changes. For example, I wanted to spend more alone time. I was going within and becoming aware of the beauty of nature, especially trees and birds. I knew there was a bigger and better future out there once I had left the family home. The ex-husband was still trying to call the shots, but it became clear I didn't have to listen to him anymore. I started instructing the conveyancing solicitor and taking control. Part of the awakening process was about reflecting on what had gone on before and choosing to do things differently.

I started seeing through the illusions regarding my ex-husband's family and their lack of acceptance of their son's actions. In 2016, I tried to explain my husband's behaviour and how damaging it was within our family. It was when my then father-in-law said, "But can you prove it in court?" and mother-in-law said: "What is domestic abuse?" that I knew they were in denial. Then there was the insincerity of my sister-in-law, who said: "I'll support both of you." However, she at least acknowledged in a phone call that she knew her brother was abusive.

The family courts have let mothers down and don't believe us even when we have proof of abuse. They mandate contact at any cost and naively believe that once we separate from abusive partners everything is solved; especially for women who have children, the abuse will stop. The perpetrators have agenda and want control by any means necessary, including weaponising their children via the mother through shared care arrangements. Unfortunately, the family courts are not trained in coercive control, nor do they really care. Awakening is seeing how things really are in the world – including how the family court system often fails to protect victims of domestic abuse.

Whilst I was married and divorcing the husband, I became aware of parental alienation. I have always had a loving relationship with our children. However, once I wanted to leave the marriage, to a toxic ex they became 'collateral damage'. Dr Amy Baker is an expert in parent relationships and uses the term to describe the complication of children being encouraged by one parent, who is the favoured parent, to unjustly reject the other parent – the targeted parent. Unfortunately, this type of behaviour is more likely to occur in separated families; she has also seen a link with a narcissistic parent.

I became painfully aware that I was experiencing parental alienation and that the family court system was not trained to spot this mental condition. They couldn't see or help targeted parents and children who are affected by this within domestic abuse, as parental alienation is part of coercive control. I had the awful realisation that the family court didn't understand the complexities of my individual situation.

Dr Amy looked at long-term studies and showed that adult children who had experienced parental alienation had trust issues; it affected their mental health and had long term effects within the family dynamic.

The intention of parental alienation is for the favoured parent to belittle the targeted parent, and to make out the targeted parent has no value to the child. It's a black and white thinking model where the targeted parent is all bad and the alienating/favoured parent is all good. Other tactics include isolation and erasing and replacing the targeted parent in the child's heart and mind. The way this is done is by allowing the child to believe they don't need the targeted parent, so they become co-dependent on the alienating parent. I had my parental authority undermined consistently over time. The targeted parent is portrayed as unsafe and unloving and children are encouraged to betray their trust. However, not all children will be influenced by these tactics. But when these signs are present and children are unable to resist the pressure, they are referred to as being alienated as they are aligned towards only one parent.

It is generally toxic people who encourage this behaviour; they actually feel good that they have achieved their objectives, as they want to win at any cost. The cost to the child is that they have to reject a part of their self, as they are made up of both their mother and father. This is what is unconscious to the toxic ex: they want to be the only thing that matters, and they are not concerned about the damage that will unfold. The alienating parent's love is based on conditional love, even if that comes at a price to the targeted parent and the child. I, on the other hand, will always have unconditional love for our children. Our children deserve compassion for being put in such a challenging situation by the alienating parent. It took me many years to figure out what had happened to me; it's even harder for children to navigate this difficult path.

I know from my extensive research that abusers don't understand the concept of co-parenting, although this is best for the welfare of children. Yet Cafcass (The Children and Family Court Advisory and Support Service) continues to recommend shared care arrangements even where there is a clear pattern of domestic abuse. This gives the green light for control (post separation abuse). The courts can't make abusers co-parent. In a narcissistic family system, the targeted parent and children need extra support, rather than suggesting legal action, which is expensive, just makes money for the courts, and doesn't help the target of the narcissist, who has an agenda of control. In fact, it often leads to further abuse. Research into shared care arrangements in Australia shows they are not beneficial when the mother feels there are safety concerns or there is domestic violence, and children are not less affected because there is 'high conflict'. It's interesting to note that the UK's Domestic Abuse Act 2021 incorporated economic abuse for the first time in history, and was based on extensive research by the Australia government, which concluded that abusers use money as a form of control within intimate relationships.

It is common for those with narcissist traits to use a person's mental health against them, especially if they have children. I was in an abusive relationship for a number of years and the fact of the matter is that if a woman is experiencing abuse, it's never good for their mental wellbeing. I spoke to a GP and they confirmed that abusers will sometimes cite a person's mental health to get leverage, especially when they are going through a divorce with children. It's a common tactic with those who have narcissist traits. The doctor explained that if your mental health is compromised, you will not have the capacity to go through a divorce. It was useful validation.

I also found out that when there is a discrepancy in income, abusers normally want to go for a shared childcare arrangement as they do not need to pay child support. I believe this system needs to change; child support should be separate from childcare arrangement orders.

Where there is domestic violence, my personal view is that a shared care arrangement can be detrimental to some children, because the abuser uses different tactics to hurt the other parent through the children with these types of orders, especially when a woman leaves an abuser. In a relationship where there has been control abusers use triangulation by passing on messages via the children rather than co-parenting, and children shouldn't feel burdened with this responsibility. It was rather telling when I asked my ex-husband what co-parenting was and he replied, "Passing on messages and info to the other parent." I knew then I had to prepare myself for what I was about to endure and navigate this unwanted situation.

In my experience, the ex has refused on occasion to co-parent, even though co-parenting is ultimately best for children in both the short and long term, and they witness the emotional harm this causes. I've had to have radical acceptance of this reality and give myself self-love. I can only control my own emotions and energy.

When I spoke to an independent legal adviser, they alleged that the Cafcass officer (court appointed social worker) in my case had not received any parental alienation training. It's offered, but it's voluntary whether they attend. What was even more surprising was I found out that the officer I spoke to was anti-mothers. After the process I really felt that the officer was biased. The Cafcass officer also didn't understand economic abuse, or coercive control.

I had good support from domestic abuse organisations, and I had an independent assessment that confirmed I was at high risk of psychological, economic and emotional abuse, yet the Cafcass officer seemed to overlook this evidence. In my opinion the risk is always there. This was a stark awakening that the system wasn't going to help me or our children. Reflecting back, my guides were actually trying to help me along the way – what were the chances of the legal adviser knowing anything about my Cafcass officer? I'm glad to know that my personal testimony and those of other women was compiled into a report by Lady Hilary Armstrong and was instrumental in strengthening the Domestic Abuse Bill in 2020 to include children as victims of domestic abuse. I believe that domestic violence is an epidemic.

Chapter Six: Into the Darkness
Wetiko and Narcissism

'We are currently in the midst of the greatest epidemic known to humanity.'

Paul Levy

The term 'Wetiko' comes from the Algonquin people of North America. To them, Wetiko is a parasitic spirit or thought form. Indigenous people knew about these malevolent spirits, and many indigenous people from around the world experienced this spirit in different ways. Colonialism, imperialism and genocide come primarily from Taker Culture, where individuals within a culture take what they want or need without caring about the consequences to the earth, or even other groups of people. They have a hostile mindset, believe in ownership and tend to eliminate any competition. Shamanism recognises that this thought form is built on the destruction and exploitation of others. Wetiko is an epidemic of greed and deception. From a shamanic viewpoint, those who are afflicted by Wetiko are actually power-empty, because it's a negative entity; people affected by Wetiko are like energy vampires. Wetiko has devastating consequences that have affected North America, Asia, Africa and South America, although it could be said that we can all be affected by Wetiko to some degree. Shamans knew it was an old spirit, so had ways of getting rid of it as it could affect a whole tribe and become an epidemic. Wetiko is about wanting more than our fair share; having a lack of compassion. Wetiko leads to very damaging results, like greed and selfishness; it becomes a virus that infects people. It is as if you are possessed. You think it is normal to exploit others for profit and to cannibalise other people, places and things, and this behaviour becomes the norm. Such consumption destroys the very planet we live on. Shamans knew the dangers of Wetiko so they also stamped it out as soon as they could see it happening.

In modern society, people have become disconnected from Mother Nature, and we have lost our soul essence, which was wild and free. Instead, we must fit into a complex world and become tamed souls rather than nurturing and allowing our true nature to be unrestricted. Society has suffered greatly from increased soul abandonment and power loss. When we domesticated ourselves as human beings, Wetiko was then able to create holes in our soul and this negative energy was able to take hold of us. Narcissists, sociopaths and psychopaths are more inclined to be infected by Wetiko than others because they are more vulnerable to these negative entities.

I made a connection between narcissists and dead spirits that are here in the physical realm. They too feed on negative energy, such as fear, and thrive on this low vibrational energy. I had to overcome the perceived fear I had towards my then husband and how I had been conditioned. At that time, I was a disempowered empath, who was also co-dependent due to my own childhood issues. Maybe the ex-husband could be transformed into a teacher who could allow my own childhood wounds to be addressed and healed? Self-love was a process I would need to work on throughout my life. I was going to find healing modalities within shamanism so I could remember my own innate power.

Paul Levy has written a book called *Dispelling Wetiko*. He states that: "Paradoxically, Wetiko both tries to destroy others' light, as it reminds them of what they've killed in themselves, while simultaneously trying to appropriate the light for themselves." Narcissists have often lost their own true soul essence because of trauma, and exist only to steal other people's energy. They are attracted to empaths, as we have lots of light in terms of compassion and we care about other people. It is in our nature to help others. Those with a Wetiko spirit lack empathy and think only of themselves. I have always had a free spirit, and empaths have that shine that is so attractive. In the end, I felt like a trapped bird in a cage. My light was truly dimmed until I saw a way out of the darkness. I had been an independent person before.

People with narcissist traits will eventually erode the very same traits they were initially attracted to, because they are like an empty vessel that needs to steal other people's energy for their own survival. An example of this was the way my ex-husband tried to take away my freedom through controlling the family finances. He also devalued my role as a mother, eroded my self-esteem and dimmed my sprit as a human being. Paul Levy goes on to say, "Those afflicted with Wetiko, like a cannibal, consume the life-force of other humans and non-humans for private purpose or profit, and do so without giving back from their own lives." By the end of the marriage, I felt drained and broken by the whole experience, and I was an empty shell of my former self.

It is no coincidence that narcissists have been likened to energy vampires as this is how they exist on a day-to-day basis. Their own soul essence, the part that makes us human, was lost many years ago, and they have no choice but to consume other people's soul energy to survive.

Emotional manipulators thrive on using power and control. In healthy family dynamics power is used to protect and empower the vulnerable, but in abusive households, power is used to control. This ensures the weaker person remains under the control and influence of the dominant one. The acronym FOG – fear, obligation and guilt – is used by these manipulators to maintain certain conditions and outcomes. These tactics also used by governments: fear and threats are used to keep people in line. When I wanted to leave my husband, he made it quite clear to me that I wouldn't see the children. He said I was crazy and that he would throw me out of the house. He was clearly saying this to keep me in line and his tight grip on the family finances was just another form of abuse. Fear was one of my biggest obstacles and was why I stayed so long in an unhealthy marriage. In 2012, I confided in a health visitor, and she gave me a card for Refuge, a domestic violence charity. I knew from that moment I was in a precarious situation.

Narcissists don't have the capacity to see how their behaviour has a negative impact on themselves and others and, if they are in a relationship, it becomes difficult for their partners. From a shamanic perspective, they are disconnected from their soul essence as they don't have empathy towards other people. Shamans know them as soul destroyers. There are several markers for narcissism, including genetic factors in that they are inherited characteristics and learnt behaviour. This is hardly surprising, as children observe the behaviour of their care givers and learn traits from individuals in families. Thus, the dysfunction is passed down the family linage.

The environment can play a big role in shaping this mental disorder as well. In the case of my ex-husband, while his father was extremely strict, his mother would heap praise on him as a child to make up for the harshness. This was something the ex-husband wanted to emulate in his own family. He was always the good cop and I was the bad cop to create alliances with our children. This is actually harmful from a psychological perspective because in a healthy partnership the two people work as a team with common objectives. Parental alienation causes wounds within the family structure and a narcissistic parent creates trauma because they want total devotion, power and control within the family home. A healthy person, no matter what the circumstances, would put the welfare of their children first regardless of the reasons for the breakdown of a marriage.

There is a neurobiological link between the brain, behaviour and thinking. It reminds me of when Lindsey Ellison talked about people who are colour blind, who can only see certain colours. Narcissists are like this as they are unable to see or feel the repercussions of their own behaviour and how it affects other people. They lack awareness of their thought forms. What was really surprising to learn is that deep down the narcissist knows something is not quite right. They seem vaguely aware of their faulty programming within their family of origin but manage to believe it was a normal upbringing. The ex-husband did have an insight when this manifested as a work issue. He knew something was wrong when no one would listen to him.

Ironically, this was how I felt within when I was living with him whilst I was married. I would try to explain how I felt about what was wrong, but he just didn't want to listen. My opinion about how money could be allocated in our household was met with laughter in my face. He said I knew nothing about money. My self-esteem was cut down and decimated until I reached the point where I thought I wasn't capable of anything. I felt worthless and of no actual value as a spouse. I will be eternally grateful to Lindsey for helping me to recover my self-esteem. The course I did opened my eyes and broke the spell I was living under with the ex-husband, as he was about to become.

The course taught me about finances, how narcissists don't co-parent, and the divorce process. It also included ways of dealing with the emotional well-being of my children and what they would experience. Lindsey said when you make the decision to leave your spouse, that is when it will be a true battle. This is when you will see the true person without the mask, because narcissists like to win at any cost. I knew then that I was going into uncharted waters but that, ultimately, I would regain my freedom. I had to dig deep into healing aspects of my own childhood and face those wounds that would be aggravated during the divorce.

Lindsey taught me that divorcing a narcissist is like preparing for war. The narcissist loves the court process and, like a hungry crocodile, uses it as a supply of energy. A warrioress knows that when going into war, there is also the possibility of death. My old self did indeed need to die, metaphorically speaking. Ultimately, I knew that a better and more authentic me was going to emerge, and the divorce was only one part of my soul's journey to reclaiming my whole being.

Chapter Seven: Mind, Body and Spirit

'The shaman does not believe in a division between the body and the spirit or between the visible world of form and the invisible world of energy.'

Alberto Villoldo

As I delved into shamanism, I discovered that the elders knew all about narcissism. It was something they had dealt with from the beginning of time. Narcissistic personality disorder is a mental health condition. These types of people have an exaggerated sense of their own importance, a deep need for attention and admiration, a void of empathy and a lack of remorse for their behaviour towards others. People who have narcissistic personality traits generally have troubled relationships.

In the Yoruba culture there is a tribe that has a word for sociopaths. They are known as cold souls – 'arankan' – who disregard others; they're selfish, uncooperative, full of malevolence and malice. Psychopathy (anti-social personality disorder) is also a mental health disorder that shows up as the inability to love or establish meaningful relationships. It includes extreme egocentricity, and manipulative and cold-hearted behaviour. Shamans would have been aware of all these types of behaviours and how they affected a tribe. In shamanic hunter-gatherer tribes, these traits would be contained and controlled to a certain extent, for 'the greater good' of the whole tribe.

A tribe needed to work together in order to survive and ultimately thrive. It made sense that to have a collaborative and high functioning tribe, any conflicts or personality differences needed to be resolved. If there was serious conflict, it would threaten the tribe. Psychopathic conduct – such as lack of empathy or disregard for others – created anxiety and fear within the tribe, so it was imperative that it be squashed and dealt with efficiently. Narcissistic, sociopathic and psychopathic traits were identified, shamed and reprimanded. The tribe held a meeting, known as a council. If the behaviour continued, the individual was thrown out of the tribe, and in essence there would be dire consequences within shamanic culture. To be isolated and sent out of the tribe was essentially to die. In this way they were able to contain this type of behaviour.

The question we have to ask ourselves now is, "Why does it seem that the modern world is run by psychopaths and narcissists who are allowed to get away with destructive behaviour?" To find the answer, we have to look back through history. Many people are unaware that there was a genocide of shamans because it is a hidden part of history. An example of this was the Salem witch hunt, where women were tortured, hung and put in prison. There were also the Cornish witch trials from 1581-1696. Anyone found guilty was executed. In 1736, the Witchcraft Act in the UK was repealed but people with 'magical powers' were still imprisoned. And then there was the 'lost' report into genocide, torture, rape and enslavement of indigenous tribes during Brazil's military dictatorship.

From 4000 BC. there was an increase in climate change. Crops were failing and people were starving as their way of living was eroded. There was a new modern era coming in the form of agriculture and the first cities were established, causing a mass exodus of people from the countryside into the cities. The lives of hunter-gathers was greatly affected. Cities were changing into city-state cultures; people were becoming territorial over land and resources. They began fighting and strategic pockets of land became huge fortresses, so people who were afraid of being attacked would feel safer. The successful tribes were those with the most aggressive leaders, who protected their scant resources. The leaders became warlords, who took more and more resources and became even more powerful. The warlords became kings and emperors, and built empires. They became ruthless and began to subjugate, kill and enslave other tribes.

For the first time in this new society there was a cultural split between men and women. Society was unequal and hierarchical and for the first time in human history we saw one group of people grab power and dominate the other. Men seized power over women and the patriarchy was born. This is reflected in the end of goddess worship, as women were now valued as objects, in terms of being chattel. There was extreme income inequality – some people were rich while others were left to literally starve in the street. The whole tribal mindset of looking after one another, caring for the ill, old and vulnerable, dissipated. People lost their independence and strength as a tribe, and a new ruling elite took over. The hunter gatherer tribes dissolved and the rulers-maintained power through oppression, torture, organised religion and terror. Tribes became races of people instead. They become 'Others'.

You can see the rise of slavery across the five habitable continents of the planet. In his book *Sapiens*, Yuval Noah Harari discusses the different mindsets and behaviours of 'Taker' and 'Leaver' cultures. If we delve deeper, there are distinct characteristics of how they treat natural resources – especially the land. The hunter-gathers were the Leavers, meaning they would only use a certain amount of land and leave the rest for animals, ensuring they had enough food for themselves. The Leaver cultures were inclined to protect the land and they treated animals and plants with respect. The Taker cultures took whatever they wanted and would also take any surplus for themselves. They had an aggressive mindset and would eradicate any real or imagined competition. The Takers were agriculturist and had no hesitation in fighting the Leaver cultures. The thought form (value system?) of the Takers was land ownership and they had no regard for animals, plants and spaces.

American Indians wept when they witnessed the slaughter of buffalo and saw farmers chop down forests and plough the land. It was like watching Mother Earth being destroyed. Leaver cultures were highly connected to the land in comparison to the Taker cultures, which had a lack of empathy or compassion for people, plants and land. And so, the divide grew between humans on the planet.

The change from living in tribes to living in agricultural settlements gave rise to day-to-day tension and stress in people's lives. Life was simple in tribes, but now there were land disputes, rigid social structures, new laws and contracts. People needed to barter and had to spend a long time looking after the land by clearing, sowing and preparing it for different uses. There were rules and regulations. People had less time to spend with their family and on spiritual matters. There was now a distinction between those who lived in a city culture and those who were more rural, the hunter-gatherers. This further divided people into 'Civilised', which had connotations of being above nature, versus those who were 'Uncivilised', who were seen as being untamed, out of control and inferior.

There was also the emergence of religions, which controlled people and encouraged them to go against their 'animal-like' natures; religion cut people away from their inner knowing. The rhetoric (dogma) of religion was focused on how the individual could not trust their natural urges or their soul. Religious experiences were dependent on what the priest told you to believe. Early churches kept the actual scriptures in the realm of only literate priests and the well-educated. This separation between people and an intimate relationship with the creator was the beginning of people losing their personal power and handing it over to others. This also created soul and power loss on a collective scale.

Chapter Eight:
Can You Hear Me?

'Your calling is buried in your background and life experience.'

Sunday Adelaja

It felt like I had always been searching for a spiritual practice. Now I knew I needed it more than at any other time in my life. I had always loved the subject of psychology, as I was fascinated with human behaviour. I enjoyed learning about different cultures and learning about social anthropology, which studies patterns of cultural meanings, including norms and values. I studied for a degree in media and cultural studies and was always fascinated by shamanic cultures; I was naturally drawn to archaeology for the same reason. I loved anthropology and learning about the roles that women played in these societies. My degree involved analysing the media in its historical, economic, social and political context. My course included examining race, gender and sexuality and how it related to everyday life, including the structures of power, economy and politics. I realised that I was inquisitive and curious about life; I wanted to know more about shamanism especially, and this was instrumental in my calling towards it.

These studies led me to delve more deeply into my own family history. I enjoyed hearing about my father's childhood in Nigeria, his time in the Royal Air Force, about the Biafra war in Nigeria, and the role of oral African history. Ironically, my father never mentioned that his father was a shaman, but he did tell me some stories about him. For example, he said that one day, when he was a young boy, his father (my grandfather) said some magic words and drank some palm wine. Suddenly the wine turned into a snake, and as my grandfather continued to talk the snake disappeared. I was blown away by this information. How strange it was that, when my grandfather died, I went on a quest to learn about shamanism without knowing that I came from a bloodline of shamans!

Through my research into shamanism, I had read about the different ways of shapeshifting. I knew it was possible to do this by journeying. In an altered state of consciousness, you can take on the characteristics of different animals. I think it's because I'm open to these ideas, but little did I know how relevant the snake was to become. It is an important power animal for me now. I have often wondered if my grandfather was somehow communicating with my dad. I knew I was going through an important transition in my life and this knowledge would be a catalyst for my calling to shamanism. It was as if I was being prepared for something bigger than myself. Wow! I was beginning to be intrigued and I knew that once I made a commitment to myself, I wouldn't be able to go back. I'd had some powerful meditations while doing reiki healings, and shamanism seemed like the next logical step. I kept that conversation with my dad alive in my mind. It seems the information he gave me was given for a reason. Maybe he knew on a subconscious level that I needed it. The ancestors have a funny way of getting information from the other side.

When my dad died, I knew I needed to answer the call of shamanism and for me, this meant a soul retrieval. I had read about them and knew I needed to confront things from my childhood. I enquired about a soul retrieval from a shaman called Narda; her grandmother was also a shaman. Ah, was that a coincidence? The universe has ways of keeping us on the right path. I had a good feeling about Narda. The snake was about to make another appearance. Narda didn't want me to give her too much information because we would discuss anything that came up after the session. I also had questions about another event from my childhood that I hadn't told many people about. I knew I needed to go back to my childhood to make peace with and heal a repressed traumatic experience. But I would have to wait and see what happened during the soul retrieval.

Spiritual paths are unique for everyone, yes, but there will definitely be helpers along the way. I spoke with my shamanic practitioner and we decided to do a distance healing session. Before she did the soul retrieval, Narda explained that she would have to ask her guides. I was really pleased about that. Ethics is an important consideration. It goes against ethics to heal someone without their prior consent because everyone has free will. This is something the creator gave to all humanity. It's important to ask our guides for permission as healing is sacred; it's a respectful thing to do. The guides are working on your behalf and everyone must be in agreement. There is only one rule in shamanism and that is to ask permission for healing.

The night before my soul retrieval, my grandfather made an appearance in a dream. He spoke to me via clairaudience and said: "The time is now." He then showed me a stick and threw it to me. I knew he wanted me to catch it and that is exactly what I did. I threw the stick to the floor and it shapeshifted into a snake and then reverted back into a stick. I threw it back to my grandfather and he vanished. I could tell he was pleased with the decision I had made. It was a powerful dream on many levels. I then had a dream about my mother. I saw my birth and she spoke to me and said she was sorry about what had happened to me; she knew exactly what I had endured throughout my life. In the spirit realm they can see the past, present and future. I felt strongly that she was proud of me. For the first time in my life, I felt pure unconditional love and I actually cried the next day. I was trying to process the information on a psychic and emotional level. I could feel the spirit of my mother and grandfather; I knew I was in good hands and I would reveal my dream to the shaman after the healing to try and make sense of it all.

I was apprehensive about confronting the other traumatic event in my life. I have no real strong memories between the ages of four and eight. When a distressing event occurs during childhood, the brain suppresses the memory as a form of protection, and this happens during soul loss. However, the body can hold onto this memory and it can then manifest as disconnection. During my marriage I had to numb my emotions because my ex-husband was so cold and emotionless. When he did show emotion, it was in the form of manipulation. An example of this was when he begged me not to divorce him and then mentioned that he would take me back even if I did. Hell would have to freeze over before I even reconsidered my decision! I found it impossible to trust him by this point. He had broken too many vows within the marriage. My instinct warned me not to tell him about this particular event from my childhood. Psychically, I knew he would use it against me. I look back and I'm thankful that I didn't tell him.

My inner calling was also foreshadowing that my life was going to be transformed as I transitioned into my new life as a single woman. This was all about putting myself first, because of the past betrayals of my true essence, and it was also for the healing of my inner child. When someone gets the shamanic call, they can take action with a power they did not know they had. You cannot ignore it or refuse to take it any further. Some people decide to put it on hold for a while, and other people decide to consciously choose the path. Your life will never be the same, and it will open up a different world to you.

Signs you might be having a shamanic calling:

- You are empathic and in touch with your emotional self and have the power to support others in your life.
- You're highly perceptive: able to read people and situations.
- You're sensitive in nature and can use all your senses to receive information.
- You enjoy solitude and can have hermit-like behaviour. You can be introverted, extroverted or an ambivert (a balance of both).
- You recognise the bigger story or picture of what's happening in the world. You want to be part of that story and able to hold a vision. You create space within yourself to do so.
- You have a calling to support others emotionally and spiritually: working or offering services in jobs such as health coach, energy healing, teaching, health services and giving advice to marginal groups or individuals.

- You have seeker energy: making the decision to embrace lifetime learning, research information and send out feeler energy to find your own truths. You will seek out alternative information (solutions) to connect with spirit and ancient arts that include plants, crystals and animals.

- You're creative and artistic, realising that this expression comes from the divine.

- You're someone who has experienced a soul initiation: you may have suffered abuse, been in a narcissistic relationship, had an illness, car accident, been hit by lightning – and these experiences make you go through a personal journey that leads to an inner understanding of yourself.

- You're a wounded healer – able to go on your own healing journey in order to heal others.

- You feel a deep connection with nature and animals.

- You're drawn to and attracted to ancient sites. You're someone who has vivid, prophetic dreams – calls from ancestors, ascended masters, guides or people who have crossed over.

Make your own notes:

Chapter Nine: Soul Parts

'Resilience is not just for surviving the worst day of your life; it's for thriving every day of your life.'

Dr Rick Hanson

The soul retrieval was about doing the inner work, doing a deep dive into my past. I had been avoiding this because I knew the process was going to be painful. I realised that my higher self was whispering to me that it was time for a deeper healing. This healing had to do with finding power through my own vulnerability. I had always had a sense of fear and lack of trust in life. The only way to overcome this fear was to confront it. I was finally ready to face those uncertainties and hesitations. I knew I couldn't go back to my old life, as it had died. This journey was about creating a new identity. With the words of Lindsey Ellison running through my mind – "This is your time to start over" – I felt like I had a second chance.

Most people are married and lead a predictable life, but when you are divorced it's an opportunity to reinvent yourself and do new things. What I loved was that I could now make my own decisions, and the soul retrieval felt like a radical act of self-acceptance that would ultimately be a positive experience along the path of healing. I had to go back to the roots of my childhood wounds and heal them.

The process began with purification. I was advised not to have any alcohol for twenty-four hours and to relax at home. I decided to ground myself by going for a walk-in nature; I knew intuitively that my life would be different, and I should begin to prepare for the transformation by getting in touch with nature.

We are all born whole and complete, and in essence we are energy. However, as we go through life, certain events shatter that energy into little pieces. The role of the shaman is to find the lost parts and integrate them back into the soul. The shamanic practitioner does soul loss work by going into a different realm (non-ordinary reality) to find the lost soul parts. The journey is like going for a walk and the shaman will see the client's history, including the soul parts that were cast out at that particular space and time.

If a therapist is working with a client, they are able to access what happened to the client in terms of the body, mind and emotions, whereas the shaman is able to get to the root of the issue through the soul. An analogy of this is going along in a car and making stops on the way: the driver (the client) sees a certain viewpoint, which becomes a memory, but the shaman is able to go to other terrains not accessible by car.

As I said before, soul loss occurs when a disturbing event happens and the soul decides to leave the body because it is too traumatic for the individual to deal with. In my case, I was sexually violated. I had only vague memories from the ages of five to eight and I really wanted to know what my inner child's point of view was. I wanted to know what she felt at the time of the event. Now I was going to go back to the hurtful past that I didn't want to deal with, for obvious reasons. As an adult, it felt like a haunting, something that was always lingering and lost in my memories, so I really wanted some validation and clarity.

The thing about memories is that they are stored away in your mind, but the trauma isn't dealt with – until you feel safe enough to handle it. A shaman can provide that safe space. By going into a trance using drums and rattles, a shaman finds and integrates soul parts that have been lost by the client. The shaman goes back into the history of the event and identifies the lost parts that need healing. While they are doing this, they will encounter their client at a certain age in their childhood and ask the child if they want the lost parts to be returned to them. The shaman will then do this by blowing into the heart and crown area of the client's head. They will ask their helping spirit to assist them in this process. Power animals can also show up as helping spirits. The representation of the child can come up in different forms within the journeying. Sometimes a soul part doesn't want to come back, for a variety of reasons. If this happens then the shaman will respect the soul part's wishes.

I decided to do long distance healing for practical reasons (Narda, my shaman, lived outside London and there was a train strike) and I arranged a date and time. I was at home and was lying down relaxing whilst it was carried out. I felt different sensations in various parts of my body throughout the healing. Thoughts were swirling in my head and I found myself crying as I felt an emotional release.

After the soul retrieval had been completed, I experienced different emotions. I felt calmer and had a sense of unconditional love that I hadn't felt for a very long time. I felt relaxed and at peace. I spoke to Narda afterwards. I had experienced two deep soul losses, first when I was sexually molested and then again when my mother died. Narda helped me to come to terms with these profound events, which had changed my life forever. She explained how I had given my power away. She said the snake was going to assist my healing, and explained that I had unending grief, and this made perfect sense. This would explain why I allowed myself to be disempowered by my ex-husband. I had gaps, or holes, in my body and I had allowed a negative energy to enter my life. From a shamanic point of view, I had weak boundaries, and this was also related to the person who violated my body. It would explain the memory gap I experienced, and why my adult self had issues with accepting the abuse as a real experience, because forgetting it was a form of self-protection.

My child self was saying, "Why didn't you tell anyone?" I believe it was to do with shame, since sexual abuse is still a taboo subject. Society has a better understanding of the lasting effects of abuse on children and adults, but it is still a sensitive subject that people find hard to talk about. There is a lasting stigma around sexual abuse. We have a long way to go as a society to provide support for rape victims and there are very low prosecution rates when this crime is committed. For me, because I was so young at the time, I didn't even have an understanding of what happened to me. I was also especially vulnerable because my mother was ill. My way of protecting myself was to not deal with it.

The shaman explained that when she did the soul retrieval, she saw a group of women who were angry on my behalf, and she informed me that with the support of these women I would never allow men to disempower me again. In order to start the healing process, I would need to have a dialogue with my inner child. Narda was able to find the two soul loss parts and integrate them back into my body. She could further see that I had two power animals. The first was a mouse. I laughed when she told me as I'm not keen on this particular animal. But when she explained the significance, and that they are known as God's little helpers, she got my attention. This power animal also represents taking action and looking at the details of things before going on to the really big matters. I could see how this interpretation correlated to my situation because I had to figure out how I wanted my life to look, post-divorce. The second power animal was the snake, which would reveal its power to me. There was also the matter of my inner child and how I had neglected myself. I needed to create self-love within me as this would ultimately help me to heal, as well as helping my children further down the road because of the damage the ex-husband had caused within the family dynamic.

Chapter Ten: Shadows

'There's no light without shadow,
just as there is no happiness without pain.'

Isobel Allende

I accepted bad behaviour directed at me. This was why I was in an abusive marriage for such a long time. I understood now that my inner child was asking the serious question "Why didn't you tell anyone?" At first, I felt upset and sad for my younger self – until I realised the connection. There was a direct parallel with the domestic abuse I experienced. There is a huge sense of shame about experiencing domestic abuse. Although there can be a greater awareness, no one wants to admit to going through this. My inner child felt misplaced shame. She was not the adult in the room; the abuser was. I can see how my younger self was still playing out in my adult self. I was in denial of the narcissistic abuse within my marriage for a long time, although

I knew something wasn't right with my husband. The abuser will always be in denial, as they wear a mask so they can be nice to the outside world and present this fake side of their personality. However, when they are carrying out the abuse, they behave completely different to the victim. The abuser is never accountable and some people in their own family often remain in denial. However, not everyone will be fooled. Someone in the family will know what they are really like.

Many years ago, in 2012, I had a powerful dream where I was walking in mud and saw a snake jump up to bite me. It was as if the snake was trying to wake me up, and as luck would have it, during my soul retrieval the shaman introduced me to my second power animal. She laughed with me about my fear of the mouse because she said she could see the snake, which was hiding in plain sight in the mud. It was right there, waiting patiently to assist me. I was starting to see all the connections with this particular power animal as well. The dream was speaking to my soul. For the snake to show up in my soul retrieval was a sign of healing and transformation.

The retrieval was only the beginning in more ways than one. I was so happy that I did it. First, it answered so many questions regarding the faulty programming within my family dynamics. I had been unconscious of somehow feeling shame, as I had internalised the sexual abuse; my childlike self wouldn't have had the words to explain what had been done to me. The emotional and psychological abuse at the hands at my ex-husband was so much clearer and I could see how he had influenced our children and created a loyalty conflict through manipulation and brainwashing. He was constantly undermining my parenting. I realised that I would need to start the journey to self-love and reparent myself. I had been betrayed by my ex-husband and I had to look at the shadow part of myself that had remained in darkness because of my traumatic childhood. I could see the burdens I was carrying.

The shaman explained that I was indeed a powerful healer. She went on to explain that my original destiny is as a seer. I always had a 'knowing' as a child that I wanted to be a healer; I had a strong intuition to assist humanity. I felt destined to be someone who has spiritual insight. I can see visions through my third eye, and I'm able to do healing in this particular way. One great aspect of shamanism is that there is always more to learn and discover.

Following this experience, my prayers had been answered. I wanted to know if I was on the right path to do my training towards becoming a shamanic healer. It turns out I was correct, and Narda could sense my doubts and uncertainties. She said it was now up to me to take the next steps towards training and learning shamanism as a spiritual practice. She told me about the army of women who were angry on my behalf for what I had experienced as a young child; Narda explained they were there in spirit, supporting me. I was advised that I would need to start to consciously reconnect with my inner child. So, I started the process of inner child work. It began with finding a photo of myself as a child to honour what she has been through. I'm learning the art of self-love and connection right back to the deepest part of myself.

The soul retrieval allowed me to face my shadows and do the inner work and that was the gift I received as I realised my super power was going through the darkness to the light, extracting the positives. The shaman also enlightened me to my unending grief and it all made sense. Something was missing within me. I had lived with a feeling of inner sadness, and for me at least, something had profoundly shifted. I felt the connection again to the little girl who felt unseen within my family of origin. She was missing her mother and didn't have the words to explain her grief. No one could see it, but I felt it always without being conscious of this feeling. As an adult, I can start to rebuild my emotional vocabulary about this grief and sadness. Once it is named, I can better heal it.

Shadow work is about working on the parts of ourselves that we do not want to see, acknowledge or accept. I had certainly been putting off doing this type of work, but my soul was telling me that now was the time to start. Throughout history, shamans knew the importance of doing shadow work because it holds the key to healing. Having a shadow side is not negative and I was about to get to know myself properly and make friends with all the facets of myself. In shamanism it is important to recognise when things are not working. My biggest wakeup call was finding the strength to leave a dangerous situation and managing the situation while living with a manipulator. Shadows can also come from past lives and unprocessed energy. The advantage of doing shadow work was that it allowed me to have unity and harmonise my lost soul parts. I was able to integrate those parts over time by creating trust from within. The path to healing is integration, and I asked the shaman what this would look like. She said that I would have to allow myself to feel all my emotions, and communicate with my inner child through self-acceptance, observing without judgement, and completing a childhood review.

Other positive aspects of confronting my shadows enabled me to tap into my deeper gifts and talents. I began to bring my shadows into the light rather than run away from them. I was finally able to support myself and build a stronger foundation for the next phase of my life. I also discovered that I was what is called an indigo child, my third eye was opened, and I discovered how different power animals could protect, guide and heal me. I discovered my natural gifts as a powerful healer. You can ask questions about your shadows and find answers when doing shamanic journeying.

Exercise: Ways to work with your inner child and shadows

- Write a letter to your inner child.

- Ask questions about your inner child.

- Use your less dominate hand to respond to questions.
- Journal about your childhood. Do a childhood review.
- What parts of yourself do you dislike?
- What parts of yourself do you judge?
- What parts do you fear?
- What behaviours and emotions were judged by your parents/caregivers?

Make your own notes:

Chapter Eleven: Travelling Without Moving

'There ain't no journey what don't change you some.'

David Mitchell

As a child, I loved the film of *The Wizard of Oz* (1939), adapted from the book by L. Frank Baum. On an unconscious level I felt like the character Dorothy, who discovered her power and self-realisation by going down the yellow brick road. To me, that film is about the journey of a truth seeker. The film is also an unconventional movie about a heroine's journey. Shamanic journeying has three main areas of focus. There is the upper world, middle world and lower word. *The Wizard of Oz* is a classic example of upper world journeying. The upper world can be described as a place that is ethereal. This word has connotations of being celestial. It is a place where angels, ascended masters and elemental beings reside and where mythical power animals can be seen and felt.

The upper world consists of compassion, love, healing and spiritual insights. According to Merriam-Webster, the ancient Greeks believed the earth consisted of four elements – fire, air, water and earth – and the heavens had a substance identified as 'ether' or 'quiescence'. Ether can be defined as invisible light or fire and in the English language in the 1500s referred to anything heavenly or airy. In Paul Francis' book *The Shamanic Journey*, he discusses how westerners see the upper world as 'above' or 'higher'. Christians interpreted the upper world as heaven and it serves as a place we ascend to. However, in shamanism, non-ordinary things are seen as quantum reality. In one way, our left brain is not really able to make much sense of this, so we see images in order to try and understand. That is where symbolic and metaphorical images come into play. When I did my first upper world journey, I could see clouds and saw spiritual guides in human form. They were wearing robes, like monks, and their faces were hidden.

Back to the *Wizard of Oz* imagery, Dorothy Gale is carried from her farm in Kansas to the magical land of Oz by a tornado. She begins a quest with her new friends, the tin man, the scarecrow and the lion, to find the wizard, who will help her to return home to Kansas and also help her friends. It is about Dorothy's journey through fear and self-doubt, where she struggles and overcomes her shadows. In the end, she is able to go back to divine source. "You had everything you needed all along…" says Glinda the Good Witch, when Dorothy asks what she needs in order to return home. The film is also about the heroine's spiritual journey.

Let us take Dorothy's name, which means 'gift of God', and that of her dog, Toto; he represents inner intuition and the name Toto means 'whole and complete'. The dog is symbolic of our animal-like nature and he is a faithful companion to Dorothy. In the film we see the ordinary reality of Dorothy living on a farm with her aunt and uncle. This part of the film is in black and white. Dorothy has received a legal notice to have her dog destroyed when it bites a woman called Miss Gulch. Dorothy is distraught by this. Then a tornado takes her all the way to the magical place known as Oz. We see Dorothy as a fearful child following her separation from her aunt and uncle. But, by the end, we see her as a fully self-realised young girl who has overcome trials and tribulations with her helpers: the tin man, who needs a heart; the scarecrow, who wants a brain; and the lion, who needs courage. These are interesting choices for guides. From a shamanic point of view, Dorothy goes from being unconscious, thinking she has no power, to a fully conscious and powerful human being. Shamanism is about being interconnected and whole, with access to the powers that self-actualisation brings. The land of Oz is where Dorothy learns lessons about herself.

In the story, she accidentally kills the Wicked Witch of the East and by doing this, she meets the Munchkins, who believe she's a witch. Glinda the Good Witch of the North gives her the magic ruby slippers that will protect her. Glinda then advises her to go to the Emerald City, where the Wizard of Oz can help her to get back to Kansas and assist her friends. The unconscious reality becomes conscious within Dorothy when she realises, she had the power to go home by clicking her shoes together three times. Dorothy understands that she doesn't need to look for happiness from the external – as in other people or in Oz – but from within herself, because that is what her heart desires. This is why she says, "There's no place like home." This is the deepest sense of the shamanic journey for me.

Lower world journeying

From a religious perspective, the lower world is often known as hell. The lower world is seen to be less than welcoming. In fact, it is seen to be bad. The lower world can also be known as the underworld and is synonymous with doom and gloom. Where did these ideas of hell and the lower world come from? In *The Shamanic Journey,* Paul Francis writes about the rise of 'civilisation' in 4,000 BC, which was actually 'the fall' when people became disconnected from Mother Nature. It was the birth of patriarchy and a city state culture. I would say that this was a bad time for women as well. They lost their power and status because women were associated with nature and the strength of creation.

The lower world is a good place to be though, because this is also where you can meet your spirit guides and power animals and find unconditional love. This world consists of Standing People (trees), Plant People, Stone People and Mother Nature, who has so much to show you – including your ancestors. This is where my healing happened in more ways than one. I found another power animal here. Panther was waiting for me and this beautiful animal showed me so much. I discovered Panther when I did my first shamanic journey and it was simply amazing. This animal continued to show up for me many other times as well. There was one particular time I needed help because I was getting so dragged down from selling the family home. I was feeling helpless and saying that my situation felt impossible. Panther just appeared in my shamanic reality and I climbed onto her back. It's important to note that power animals can communicate telepathically with you. Whilst in the shamanic realm I was saying to myself that my current everyday reality felt impossible. Panther replied: "Impossible? I'll show you what I can do." Panther just walked up to me and I held on tightly as we jumped through the sun. It's ironic when you think about it, as the word 'impossible' is also 'I'm possible'. I did a power animal dance and I could feel myself take on the characteristics of this powerful animal. In shamanic reality, Panther was able to do anything in this particular realm.

The sun is symbolic of alchemy and will power and is a life force energy. We need the sun for plants and food and it gives us vitamin D. In essence, the sun also represents feminine power. The panther as an animal is about death, rebirth and courage. This animal is an ancient and strong spirit guide. It is not surprising to me that it chose to be my power animal. I felt so much fear around letting go of the family house because my future was as yet a big unknown. The panther was helping with that fear and uncertainty. I have so much gratitude for this power animal.

The lower world is where you are able to lay the foundations towards healing with Mother Nature as she is nourishing; this is where you can start your own personal growth. You can lay the strong and solid foundations to withstand any adversities. This is the power of going to the lower world.

Middle world journeying

The middle world is a completely different matter. You could say that the middle world is where hell resides, because it operates on different rules and is very complex. The upper and lower worlds are safe places to be, as nothing bad will ever happen there. They are filled with so much wisdom and healing, unlike the middle world, which is full of dangerous people, abuse, murder… It is not a nice place. There is beauty in the middle world, and kindness and compassion. However, you have to have personal and collective boundaries when doing a middle world journey. The middle world can be a dangerous place because this reality includes deception and people who do not have your best interests at heart. There are rules, injustices, inequality and all manner of things that are negative and cause distress and harm. It is a place of complex social constructs that are real but also illusionary in that someone made them up and accepted them as the status quo. This world is physical and energetic; it has a vibration that can feel good or bad. As Paul Francis describes eloquently, in the middle world we may experience the image in our mind's eye of getting a 'knife in the back'. Sometimes you may tune in to someone who you suspect has a dark energy, and it will be confirmed by seeing a dark cloud.

Middle world journeying is useful for dealing with negative energies and possessions. It must always be done with caution as it can be a frightening process. When I did a middle world journey, I discovered that I had actually met my ex-husband in a past life. My higher self then advised me to do a cord cutting to release all attachments. I have done meditations and had visions where I met my ex-husband in a previous lifetime.

Shamanism is about removing the veils that keep human beings in ignorance. Paul Francis says, "Shamanism is sometimes described as a process of 'waking up' and facing things as they really are. Shamanic middle world journeys are an essential part of shamanic healing, in terms of dealing with unhealthy energies, possessions, unhealthy entanglements, soul loss and so on."

Chapter Twelve: Black Panther

'The nature of panther is that he never attacks. But if anyone attacks or backs him into a corner, the panther comes up to wipe that aggressor or that attacker out.'

Huey Newton

Panther came in really handy when I was having to face my ex-husband in court regarding the house. I disliked courts because they have a really low vibe energy and they are not the best place for a woman to feel empowered or for her voice to be heard. I did a shamanic journeying a few days beforehand to give me courage and strength and Panther showed up again. By the time I went to the court, I felt calm. I knew exactly how the ex would try and play out the situation. I walked in with confidence; I had asked my guides to protect me and to be given a decent judge. As usual, the ex-husband greeted me on the offensive. This act struck out at me immediately within a couple of minutes of going into court. It was a tactic to throw me off guard. This is typical narcissist behaviour, since they want to get one over you to keep you off balance and scattered and induce panic. But this time the tactic was going to fall flat. I briefly looked over it and put it to the back of my mind; I knew I wouldn't need to refer to made-up lies. I actually laughed to myself because I knew his game so well.

So, I felt really relaxed when I entered the courtroom. As usual, he tried to dominate the proceedings, yet I felt calm and relaxed. The calmer I was, the more irate the ex-husband became, and the judge became obviously annoyed by his conduct. The ex-husband went into attack mode and said I was delaying the house sale. I calmly gave verified facts, to which he whined like a toddler. At one point the judge and I just exchanged looks and both of us raised our eyebrows. The judge had the look of having seen these type of men a hundred times.

"I want to have sole conduct," the ex-husband said, regarding the house sale; we currently had joint conduct in the court order he had agreed to. The judge stonily reminded him several times that he would need to put in an application to get the court order changed. "I will need to move back into the family home," he said. I thought to myself, *Oh no, that's not happening*. His relationship with a woman couldn't have been going too well. The ex-husband was now trying to plead poverty on a salary of over fifty thousand pounds a year, as he was renting, and he thought the house sale was going too slowly.

The judge looked at the financial consent order. "It is a very strange order," he said. I agreed that it was really odd, because of the terms. Suddenly there was silence from the ex-husband. He had dictated the terms and my solicitor had informed me that there was no point in contesting everything the ex-husband had stipulated, with all the clauses and sub-clauses. Any judge reading it would summarise that it was written by a controlling dictator. However, he was still demanding that the judge make it a sole conduct. He still wanted to have control, and it wasn't going his way compared to previous occasions. The judge deliberated. "Let's see, I'm going to be free in July, but I'm busy until then." He smiled as he said this, and I was ecstatic since that was seven months away. It meant I had joint decision-making with regards to selling the house. The ex-husband looked dejected and annoyed at this point.

Things had changed for me because I no longer felt fear; for the first time, I felt full of courage. This wasn't about winning anything but about showing him that I was in charge of my life now. That freedom felt pretty amazing to me. I wasn't the same person and I wanted him to see that he didn't have a hold over me anymore. I was an independent person in my own right. I felt the spirit of Panther energy fill that court room.

EXERCISE: Power Animal Journeying

You can drum or use a recording. I like Sandra Ingerman's work: there are many options available online. It is really a matter of listening and finding drumming that resonates with you.

Take a few deep breaths. It is good to set an intention or focus for the journey. Perhaps your focus is on a question you have. Then imagine yourself going down into Mother Earth. Imagine a tree and go deep into the roots of that tree. This pathway is also known as the World Tree and is where all things are connected. You will need to keep going down and looking for an opening past the roots of that tree until you have arrived in the lower world.

Ask yourself for a power animal to appear and to show you what you need to know.

Questions you can ask:

- What can you show me?
- How can I heal …?
- What do I need to know about?

Then observe and feel everything.

Once you have completed the journey, it is good to write

everything down.

The experience will be different for everyone.

Don't worry if nothing happens. It may take practice and you can always try again.

Chapter Thirteen: Ghostbusters

'In the spirit world, there is no time as we know it. Past and future do not exist. All "time" is now.'

James Van Praagh in *Ghosts Among Us*

Whilst I was going through the divorce in 2016-2018, some strange paranormal events were occurring in the family home. These events increased in the summer of 2018 when the house was put on the market. After going through the court process with our children, we came to an agreement to have a shared care arrangement. This meant both parents would share time with our children under the same roof and once we both had separate homes. I can only say it was something I had to live with for the sake of our children.

The ex-husband eventually moved out in the summer of 2018. I realised he wanted to maintain control. In 2017 he had demonstrated he wanted to further exert his power over me by saying he would live in the house until it was sold. He tried to manipulate me by telling me I needed to move, but I played him at his own game by saying that since I wasn't working, he could pay my rent. So, he finally saw sense and moved out, once an agreement was put in place for how the house would be sold.

In an ideal world I wanted the children to have the security of being in the family home. But I realised that, in order to cut all contractual ties with my ex-husband, I would agree to the house sale. He was threatening to take it to a final hearing – narcissists love court, as it energises them and they don't care about wasting money. This is what happens when you divorce a narcissist: they want you to pay and will happily request this in front of the children. I felt more sadness for our children, who were aged twelve and seven at the time. The house held bittersweet memories and I knew it was time to let go. To me, this was a step towards reclaiming my freedom. I had never felt at home here because of the domestic violence. The house represented false insecurity. It didn't feel like a sanctuary in the way home might to other people.

As an empath, I had always sensed that there was a spirit in the house. Items would go missing without explanation. My daughter said that a cup fell off a cabinet by itself, and when she was in the bathroom a cup mysteriously ended up on the floor and smashed.

I invited my friend and psychic Lucy to our house, and as soon as she walked in, she said there was an old woman here. I recalled that there were often noises coming from the loft but I just assumed they were coming from my next-door neighbour. But Lucy could actually see the form of an old woman in a rocking chair. She was angry and bitter, but she meant us no harm. I decided I would need to deal with the situation directly because my daughter was now refusing to stay in the bedroom where these events occurred.

My gift was about to come in handy as I realised that the spirit was actually stuck in the land of the living. Unbeknownst to me, I was to carry out a ceremony known as psychopomp. This would normally require special training as it's an advanced shamanic practice, used to help an individual who has died by assisting their soul to move into the afterlife. But I confess that this was no new idea to me. I used to enjoy watching a programme called *Paranormal Investigation*. Watching this programme, I was intrigued by the empaths and how they could give the owners of a house information about stuck souls. These were souls who thought they were still alive, living in their old home. I began to formulate a plan for what could be done.

A few days after Lucy came to the house, my intuition told me to go to my regular reiki group meeting. I noticed that my usual teacher wasn't available that day. Instead, an intuitive healer would be taking the class. It felt as if my guides were assisting me. We waited to see if anyone else turned up but no one did. I had the perfect opportunity to ask her about my predicament. She calmly explained that someone I knew had called the old woman back to her home. To say I was shocked was an understatement. Who – and why would they do this to me? I put those thoughts to the back of my mind, as I concentrated on how I was going to carry out the ceremony. The healer informed me that the old woman was angry and needed to be removed from the house. I was hesitant, because I had never done this before. Would I be able to move the spirit into the afterlife? I had to keep reminding myself what the shaman had said to me: I'm a seer and a powerful healer.

I made up my mind that I was ready for the challenge. With the guidance of the healer, I gathered myself for the ceremony. I collected together white candles, white sage and Epsom Sea salt. I called upon my spiritual guides; I knew I would need to overcome any doubts that I felt. I was going into the realm of the unknown. The healer was so calm about it that I knew I would be able to do this with ease and grace.

On the day of the ceremony, I prepared myself by cleansing myself and the house with sage. The intuitive healer said my aura was murky and I realised this was due to my ex-husband's negative energy, which had built up around my energy field.

I set out the candles around me and asked my guides to be there with me. Suddenly, I felt something. I knew the old woman was watching me. I opened up to her energy and communicated with her using clairaudience. I asked her a few questions and waited for the answers. I knew I would have to gently negotiate on her behalf to get her to go towards the light. My third eye started opening and I saw a ray of white light as I beckoned her to cross over. I had a conversation with her and assured her that people she knew would be waiting for her. Although she was hesitant as she wanted to stay, I firmly explained why she couldn't hang around anymore. It took a while, as she was attached to the house, but eventually the old woman crossed over, and I knew she had gone. I felt a sadness for her, because I could feel her resistance. She was having to let go, and I realised that I too would have to let go soon. I was preparing myself to leave the house. It was a good lesson in detachment to things that no longer resonated with me. Energy is stored in the fabric of houses, and when I first viewed the house all those years ago, I knew there was sadness there. Now the previous occupier had finally let go. Perhaps I could as well.

The following day was even more surprising. I had arranged for a British Telecom engineer to look at the phone line, which was faulty. As soon as the engineer came in, he said: "I don't believe it. This is the old woman's house." He went on to explain that when he was a young boy, he visited this house as his mum was best friends with its resident, a woman called Patricia, and he had fond memories of being here. He hadn't been back to the house since he was a child, and it was a trip down memory lane for him to be back here now. I figured it must have been the same woman's spirit making her presence felt. It was as if the old woman was having the last laugh in this really peculiar situation and didn't want to be forgotten. I think she was secretly pleased that she had managed to conjure that event. It seemed the engineer could sense something as he said, "I guess people get attached, don't they? I mean, what are the chances of that happening? Some things are a complete mystery." It was as if he had an attachment to the house and knew that Patricia had died here and was still here in some form; when people die, they leave a part of their consciousness behind, including their feelings and emotions. For some reason I didn't tell him about what I had done, as I wanted the engineer to leave with those positive memories of the old woman, and I think he felt her spirit in that house. I was silently in awe of the divine intervention that occurred in that strange moment. As I reflected on my own forthcoming departure, it was a reminder that the good memories will still remain.

After that, the house's energy changed and I knew the old woman had really gone. There were no more negative incidents but I felt she was watching from afar. My daughter mentioned that the energy was lighter in the house. Ah, what a relief. I had discovered that I could be courageous despite my initial concerns about carrying out the psychopomp, and I knew I wanted to learn more about shamanism on a practical level. I had the information that the shaman had sent me and even more amazing coincidences were happening to assist me.

Whoever called in Patricia didn't realise the power I had to protect myself now that I had completed the soul retrieval. When I had originally seen the intuitive healer, it felt like I was meant to meet her. She told me that I had indeed cut the cord that connected me to my ex-husband and said he was disconnected from his own soul. The healer was able to give me insights I hadn't been consciously aware of. When I thought about my soul retrieval, I could see how my child-like self had been operating in my marriage. Now that had ended, I was free. I was finally growing up and taking responsibility. I was more able to stand up to my now ex-husband.

Before he left the house, one of his parting digs was, "You need me in this house." Bloody understatement of the century!

I just looked him in the eye and said, "Oh no, I don't need you. In fact, you need me." You see, he needed me as his narcissist energy supply – but that was about to come to an end. He wasn't going to be able to feed off my energy anymore. His tricks simply weren't working. He had lost his power and hold over me and he wasn't liking that one bit.

Chapter Fourteen: The Shining

'We need to be willing to let our intuition guide us and then be willing to follow that guidance directly and fearlessly.'

Shakti Gawain

Intuition is the ability to understand something without conscious reasoning. I have always been sensitive to the energies in my environment. I have learnt how to trust and have faith in my intuition so it benefits me, and I have had to practise this and learn the hard way because in the past I didn't always follow my intuition.

Sincc I was a child, I've always had a keen intuitive ability, but I didn't understand what it meant. It was only as I got older and I had all these experiences of being able to intuit certain things about people that it began to make sense. I was also highly sensitive as a child. I would feel things in a different way, especially music and the vibrations of sound. They would turn into colours and images before my eyes. When I was young, I went to Jamaica, and I wanted to help all the stray dogs that were injured. Wanting to help animals came from my highly developed empathic feeling towards creatures in need. I could feel their pain on a physical level and felt an innate need to assist them. I believe all these things were helping to raise my vibrations (energy) to higher psychic abilities – what is known as 'the clairs'. It is important to know that we are all born with these abilities but the world we live in is very 'left brained'. This logical world is run on logic, rational thinking and a 'seeing is believing' ideology. The right brain is all about non-reality, being creative, thinking outside the box and intuition. Believing is seeing. The clairs are accessed from the right-thinking brain. It is said there are five senses, but there is also a sixth sense. The word 'clair' comes from the Latin word 'clarus', which denotes clear, shining, and bright.

The Four Clairs

Clairvoyance

Clairvoyance means 'clear seeing'. This modality is visual, rather like the way in which you would imagine a daydream or an image in your mind's eye. When I see things before, they actually happen, it is like seeing images that come to life. I had an experience of this when my youngest child had an accident. I could see the image really clearly in my mind's eye. I had an image of my son on his scooter, and then falling head-first with blood on his face. Sometimes I see images that make no sense because they are symbolic, and I need to decipher the actual meaning. I also have visions of past lives and people.

It is important to note that I have had visions of past, present and future events. I did a meditation and saw images of myself as a child, playing with a young girl. We were separated and I was really upset by this, and I knew that I would meet my friend again. I later realised that the girl was indeed my good friend Lisa. I first met her in 2001 when we worked together in the same office for a shirt-making company. We were there for a few years and vowed to keep in touch. She now lives in Australia and has Aboriginal heritage. I told Lisa that on an unconscious level it seemed like I had known her forever. Lisa later confirmed that she'd had the same dream. We always joke that we are soul sisters. I feel as if I have met her before, and I trust her with my life.

Claircognizance

Claircognizance means 'clear knowing', like an instant download of information. Claircognizance gives me vital information; the only downside is that there is no logic to it, so it is hard to explain to other people.

Here's an example of an occasion when this happened to me. When I was still married, we were invited to go to Spain for a wedding but my intuition was telling me not to go; I had a feeling something bad was going to happen. My husband was annoyed and threw an ironing board in my direction when I suggested not going. I was so scared that I agreed to go to keep the peace. I decided to fly to Spain a few days later than him because the less time I was around him, the better it would be for me. I landed in Spain and he didn't bother to meet me; I tried to call him but his phone was turned off. Luckily, I was travelling with his friend. Unfortunately, things went from bad to worse. My husband was 'golf crazy' and had taken our son out golfing. Our son suffered really bad sunstroke and ended up in hospital. It was a complete nightmare. Thank goodness there was a lovely woman there, a friend of the bride and groom, who spoke fluent Spanish. She was able to translate and spoke to the doctors and nurses on my behalf. I was so relieved to go home, and I knew from that day on I would never travel abroad again with my husband.

Clairaudience

Clairaudience is hearing information in a non-physical frequency. This also has to do with being in communication with other beings from the non-reality realm. For example, when I was in the process of breaking up with my then husband, he said that it would be a 'bad idea' to get a divorce as he was in love with me. I suddenly heard the spirit of my brother Christopher, who said I was not to believe my husband as he was manipulating me. That was interesting, because the next day I received a call from my friend Lucy, the psychic, who said that my brother Chris had told her my husband was going to manipulate me. I laughed silently to myself as it was perfect validation.

Clairsentience

Clairsentience means 'clear feeling', and this is when you can feel vibrations in your body that give you indications of information about a situation, person or issue. An example of this was when I saw a photo of my ex-husband's father. I had a really bad feeling in my stomach. The phrase 'gut reaction' is a great example of clairsentience, because it is a natural instinct that is often there for our safety. A lack of trust in our own feelings can be explained by a lack of confidence in ourselves. Sometimes it is easier to lie to ourselves because we don't want to be disappointed with people, or situations that we find ourselves in.

From my personal experience I can honestly say I paid a high price for not acting on my intuition. I began to realise that I was married to someone with a controlling nature, and I had a father-in-law with disturbing personality traits. Let's go back to the car incident with the ex-husband's parents, when the father berated the mother because she made a mistake with the directions. At the time I was shocked; I couldn't imagine my future husband ever speaking to me like that. Oh boy, was I wrong, because I was also spoken to in a similar manner. It was a horrible realisation that my husband was indeed just like his father, although he had obviously disguised that from the very beginning of our relationship. The body never lies.

How to Access the Clairs

Some people view a psychic as someone with special gifts. This is not true, as everyone has the ability. It is just that most people have forgotten how to access it because of the way our society leans more towards left-brain thinking. The two sides of our brain work in different ways. The left hemisphere deals with order, facts, linear thinking, writing, mathematics, verbal reasoning, logical and analytical thinking, while the right-hand side is more visual and creative – it includes daydreaming, music, holistic thinking, reading emotions, empathy, art, and less organised ways of thinking. Some people lean towards either left or right brain thinking, and others will use a bit of both. We all have the potential to be 'whole-brain' thinkers.

The left brain deals with the physical, separateness and self, while right-brain thinking is non-linear and has a metaphorical approach that is more shamanic in nature. At one point in society, most people lived a shamanic way of life. We have simply forgotten how to think in this way and have become a far more left-brained society. This type of thinking is based on facts and words. Some neuroscientists might argue against the so-called brain hemispheric dominance, while others believe that we live in a left-brain-dominated society. I think it is dependent on culture and within individual people. From my own experience, I would say I am more right-brain dominant as I have high intuition, am good at reading emotions, am empathic and have been able to focus on my psychic ability as it leads me to being able to trust my own intuition. I enjoy activities that favour right-brain activities on a day-to-day basis. I feel that left-brain dominance is revered in modern society, which became more structured during the rise of industrialisation. So many systems are now in place compared to a simple hunter-gatherer society that would have naturally leaned towards a right-brain dominance. This would have been the natural way to be in a shamanic culture. I think people will try to go back to a more balanced and healthier way of life.

The great feature of clairs is that anyone can practise using their psychic abilities. However, human beings have been programmed to have an external locus of control and value logic and science over internal intuition. Meditation is one way of allowing the mind to let go and relax, and it teaches you to be able to listen and tune in to your own intuition. Remember, everyone has this ability, but it will depend on your motivation for wanting this connection. It will require patience and focus.

A good way of strengthening the clairs is by practising meditation as it allows the mind to calm down and focus on the task at hand. When the mind is like an empty vessel, you will be able to get the information you need. If you are distracted by the noise and static of day-to-day life or have everyday worries, it is harder to do. This is because you will find it a challenge to know if it is wishful thinking or not. You may have doubts because you may not get any clear information. The shaman knew that you had to keep your ego outside the door. The ego is a part of us that lives in a physical reality that is known as a middle world construct, consisting of our personal identity and sense of self. It is also made up of thought-forms, entanglements with other people, what people say to us, our belief systems, the masks we wear as well as the stories we tell ourselves.

Accessing the clairs and our higher self needs a clear mind that is free from worry and fear of the future, or what may come up for you. Trust and faith are things that are developed over time. It is about getting curious about things and investigating ourselves.

Accessing the Clairs

One way of doing this is by relaxing with meditation. The information we want and need is out there in the universe. If I have a question that needs answering I am able to sometimes directly ask my guides, and they will sometimes show me through visions in my dreams, or through my feelings. When I meditate, I find that information is more likely to come to me without having to worry about the issue or outcomes of problems. Normally I will be divinely guided. Being able to access your natural psychic abilities requires a clear mind that is free from everyday mundane distractions in order for information to flow into your mind.

Meditating is all about being in tune with your body and creating awareness. When you create awareness by focusing on your breath, your next job is just to observe what is happening in your body, for example. You will need to use your imagination to find your serene place. It could be a beach, or any happy place you find relaxing that resonates with you. You may want to sit in a chair or lie down. Create space where you can be comfortable. This works best if you can be in a location where you will not be disturbed.

You want your mind to have quietness so your innate intuition can focus on the task at hand, and meditation will allow you to be in a relaxed state. Make sure phones are turned off and you are in a quiet place.

Next, have a question for your higher self or guides. Before you do the meditation, think of something you would like help with. You will need to begin with a clear question that you would like a specific answer to, perhaps help with your relationship, health or career. I have provided some examples:

- What do I need to know about my career path?

- How can I prepare for …?
- How can I heal my body?
- What will my new life be like? (This is good for any life transition.)
- What do I need to know about?
- How can I heal my relationship with …?

Chapter Fifteen: Trusting Yourself

'Feelings can come and go like clouds in a windy sky. Conscious breathing is my anchor.'

Thich Nhat Hahn

Did anything happen when you did the meditation exercise? If you drew a blank, this could be for many reasons, such as not being relaxed. Sometimes it helps to imagine a tree.

Sometimes people see or hear something but it doesn't make any sense. Think about how you felt and let your intuition guide you.

Advantages and Challenges of Clairvoyance

Pictures can come as images and be symbolic. If you are finding it challenging to know what it means, you can ask your guides or your higher self to show you in a different way. You can ask for clarity. So, you can decide on a pre-set image and say: "I would like you to show me an image of a tree," or any image that resonates with you, and then ask questions. Keep practising, as the more you do this, the easier it will be until it becomes second nature.

If I have a question that I need answering, sometimes I will ask my guides to show me in a dream. This is a good way of finding out information, as you are in a relaxed state. You can then do another meditation and go through a process of elimination to get to the root message behind the image.

Advantages and Challenges of Clairaudience

When you first try to communicate to your guides it may be difficult because you are not yet holding a high enough frequency. If you are distracted, you won't be able to receive the message, or you may question the information. Your guide will only give you information that you need to know and information that you ask about.

Clear hearing has some real value because you can get direct answers. There are no images or pictures that need to be deciphered. A good way to strengthen this clair is to go for a walk to attune yourself to your higher self. Have a short dialogue with your guide. Ask questions that require a quick yes or no answer, and then move on to longer questions that you need answers to.

When you feel at ease, formulate your question. It will come to you from your guides, as they only want the best for you. Yes, they will warn you as well, and then intuitively you will know it is for your highest good.

I once had a strong warning from my guide. I informed my husband that our marriage was over. At first, he was calm. My intuition was amplified as I knew it was the calm before the storm. My guides said to get my key and phone and get out of the house. I listened, and had a small bag hidden by the window in the hall. He started getting angry; he kicked the table and punched the wall. He made a veiled threat and his eyes went black with rage. I immediately grabbed my bag, left the home, got help and only re-entered once it was safe to do so and I had an exit strategy in place.

The most dangerous time for a woman is when she leaves an abuser. If you are in harm's way it's better to leave as soon as possible and get specialist help from a domestic violence organisation, as they can do a risk assessment.

Advantages and Challenges of Clairsentience

The advantage of clairsentience is that you can get clear signals without any other evidence. If you are empathic, you are more likely to trust the information you pick up. However, if you are unsure about your feelings after doing the meditation it may well mean that you are getting conflicting information, and this is about not being able to trust what you feel. One of the aspects of clairsentience is that you don't have much to go on apart from your gut feeling. If you are fearful about the guidance, you are getting then the information will not be clear. It is a good idea to use other clairs, such as clear knowing, and drill for deeper information that way. However, this particular clair still has its uses, especially if you need to make a 'yes' or 'no' decision.

Ask for what you truly want and notice the feelings that come up in your body. What type of feeling do you get about different situations? Make sure your body is relaxed before asking any further clarifying questions. This is an important step, as you want the guidance from the guide to come to you for the best possible outcome. Your body will send you clues, and it is up to you to see what comes up. You may well need to use clairaudience and clairvoyance to see why you are getting any particular sensation in your body about a person or situation. Clairsentience is one of the easiest clairs to practise and it can be used every day. The more intuitive work you do, the easier it will be to connect with your guides.

I used it when I was looking for a flat. I had a time limit to find a flat and was getting disheartened after one place I fell in love with had fallen through. I meditated on the help that I was going to receive and gave it to the universe. I felt a sense of calm and relaxation about the process. The next day I noticed a flat that was in my budget, and was in my desired location. The flat had literally appeared twenty-four hours after I asked my guides for help. That flat was mine within a week.

Advantages and Challenges of Claircognizance

This clair is another powerful modality that can be used to get instant information. However, it does have its drawbacks, as you will need to have discernment around any questions you have regarding the information you receive. Is this going to be useful for me? What will happen if I do this or that? Why should I go here? Why should I do that? Claircognizance is one of the more challenging clairs to master because it requires a high vibration and to get to this level the conscious thought will need to be turned down so you can get the download. It is a bit like tuning into a radio station – all interference needs to be eliminated so you can find the right frequency and listen to the correct station. The right conditions will need to be met first to increase your vibration. A good thing to remember is that once you master the other clairs, clear knowing will become easier to access.

To get into a higher vibration, imagine you are at the bottom of a staircase or tree and you are going to climb up into space, and count for up to two minutes. You can sit down or stand up whilst doing this meditation to increase your vibration. The most important thing is to be comfortable. Personally, I find seated is best when encouraging an altered state of consciousness – some people can get light-headed and fall over if they are standing and locking their knees, for example.

It is a good idea to practise meditation daily and to persevere, as the process cannot be rushed. It will be worth it as you will feel empowered by what it can do for you.

My own experience of this particular clair will stay with me. I am attuned to them more than ever, as I now make a conscious effort to listen to them. I had an inner knowing that I would need to trust myself and my guides. My grandfather came to me once again in a dream and again said: "The time is now." In my dream he was trying to communicate information. I had an inner knowing that he was giving me news about my father. Two days later, I received the news that my dad had passed away.

I also received claircognizant advice that I was to go within, spiritually. Before I moved into my flat in 2019, my guides informed me that I would need to 'go within' and trust myself and my guides. I asked them for more guidance. Would I need to become like a hermit, metaphorically, to go within and contemplate my inner life? They said I would.

I understand now that my guides were trying to prepare me for what was to come in the year 2020. They were absolutely right;

they were trying to prepare me for something that was going to affect society on a global scale: a mass global lockdown.

Meditation Practice to open up to your clairs

Take a few deep breaths through your nose and breathe out through your mouth. Do this a few times so you are able to establish a calm rhythm.

Keep breathing throughout the meditation until you feel yourself being in a calm state. Now you will feel fully relaxed. Pause.

Focus on your feet. Feel them getting heavy and relaxed. Pause.

Now bring your focus to your lower legs and calves. Let your legs go limp and heavy. Relax your muscles. Pause.

Now focus on your knees. Remember to keep breathing and feel your knees and thighs becoming heavy, full and relaxed. Keep breathing. Pause.

Focus on your pelvis, stomach, chest and back. Take some deep breaths and release any tension in these areas. Pause.

Now focus on your shoulders, arms and hands. Let them feel full and relaxed. Pause.

Finally, move your attention to your neck and head. Breathe in and out and let go of any tension you may have here. Release all tension in your body. Pause.

Focus attention on your face and release any tension. Remember to continue your meditative breathing.

Now you need to focus on your serene place. Choose a place that resonates with you.

Once you are in your ideal place, ask your guides a question about your life and let them show you a scene. Watch what happens.

Let the scene play out and thank your guides for what they have shown you. Pause.

When you are ready, open your eyes and write down what you received and your thoughts about it.

Make your own notes:

Chapter Sixteen: Guiding Lights
The Gift of Fire

'The more you glow, the more you grow,
your light is your gift to this world.'

Indigo Ocean

I learnt so many lessons about myself by exploring what I endured during my childhood and later in my marriage. I also had to deal with my father's death at the same time I was divorcing my husband. Living with a high conflict husband – that experience would make you crumble or make you stronger. With hard work and self-exploration, I gained back my self-respect, and I learnt how to have more compassion for what my children were going through. I was able to plan how I would assist them in their own healing in the future.

Shamanic journeying held the keys to discovering my inner

strengths of fortitude. The sun that I saw in my lower world journey felt like a shamanic burning. I had a feeling of oneness with the universe as I went through the sun. It was a moment I will never forget. I felt my ancestors watching this sacred moment. It felt like a purification by fire.

I felt a level of faith and trust within myself that had been lacking during my childhood, and I was able to reclaim those gifts to create a new chapter for my life post-divorce. I realised that was one of the lessons I still had to learn. I was secretly scared of the power I had, maybe because I had seen and experienced the abuse of power by my ex-husband.

This thought resonated when I attended another shamanic workshop and the facilitator said: "Controllers are power empty." This made me think deeply about the abuse because the root cause is an imbalance of power. Then I thought about the other women who have come before me and how they were not allowed to speak their truths. Society left women vulnerable when they felt disempowered and disconnected from their strengths.

Along with the mouse, snake and panther there were other helpers from ordinary reality. On every heroine's journey there are helpers along the way, and one of mine was Nick. I met him about twenty-five years ago through a friend. He was an artist in the truest sense of the word. He saw beauty in the everyday and was one of the most authentic people I've ever known. He was a true friend and I miss him every day. Sadly, Nick died before I started writing this book, but I always wanted him to be part of my story. I wanted him to be included in my own happy ever after.

Life can be so cruel. I had images of us gallivanting around London. While I was still going through my divorce and was utterly depressed by the long process, Nick was there. When it felt like things would never end, he would surprise me with a wonderful high tea at a swanky hotel. He wrote reviews for hotels and restaurants. I remember crazy nights in Hoxton before it was 'cool', going to Dazed and Confused parties, having coffee and putting the world to rights. He suited my Indigo free spirit, and we saw the world in a similar way. He had a colourful life. I found his skills in photography fascinating, plus he wrote excellent magazine copy to go with his great photos. He was like a wise monk at times, giving sage advice, and then he could get totally annoyed by my ex-husband's crazy antics. I miss our chats in the coffee shops, and phone calls about nothing in particular. He represented safety, because I trusted him and knew he had my back. It was an honour to support him while he went through treatment for his illness.

When he was most ill, I carried out a shamanic healing for him. I blew into his heart chakra because I knew the treatment was causing him pain. It was good to know that afterwards he wrote a poem about love, and that the healing had really cheered him up emotionally. I think he knew he was going to die, even when he was talking about living on a cruise ship forever. I was confused at first. This didn't make sense because he had a flat. Then I realised he knew his time on earth was coming to an end, and he was trying to say goodbye. He passed away a couple of days later. I miss him so much. I could talk to him about anything and loved our walks on Hampstead Heath. Nick was gracious with his time and an excellent listener. He was consistent with his love, and understanding of what I was going through.

Before Nick died in 2020, I moved into my new flat. I decided that I wanted to tap into my creativity and revisited the book *The Artist's Way* by Julia Cameron. Since the whole country was in lockdown, I took an online class. As luck would have it, I met the wonderful teacher and facilitator Andrea, who is also a sound healer based in the Vale of Health in North London. It was an interesting coincidence that she lived so close to my long-time friend, Nick. The universe was working its spiritual magic once again.

I was connecting the dots because Nick's ex-girlfriend Romilly, who is also a dear friend of mine, first introduced me to *The Artist's Way* book. I smiled to myself as I was sure that Nick was looking out for me on the spiritual realm by then. Things always happen in cycles and since I wanted to reconnect with my inner child, the creativity used as a spiritual practice did just that.

Andrea was really instrumental in allowing me to reconnect. I loved hearing those infamous words "It's all about playing. Don't be so serious." Andrea is one hell of a creative soul and has a lovely playful curiosity about creativity and life in general. She is an amazing storyteller and helped me to tap into my creativity. I think it worked because I finally gave myself permission to do Artist Playdates and connect with my inner child – who really wanted me to play and get creative.

One of the other tools in *The Artist's Way* is Morning Pages. This is three pages of longhand writing that acts as a gateway towards your creativity so you gain insights into your life. Writing Morning Pages is a great way to access right-brain wisdom and activate your stream of consciousness. They are not meant to be works of art because you simply write about whatever happens to be in your mind. Our minds are usually quite full and in need of emptying.

Everyone needs an Andrea in their life, and she offers amazing sound bath healing sessions as well as Zoom classes. In 2020, I attended a picnic in her garden with other participants on *The Artist's Way* course, and it was great to be in Hampstead Heath again. I couldn't help noticing a beautiful black butterfly that was hovering around me. It felt symbolic of my own magical transformation. I could feel Nick watching over me, just like that butterfly. I also saw an actual mouse in the garden while we were eating our picnic – and this time I wasn't scared. I was rather intrigued, as it reminded me of my soul retrieval. It was one of my first power animals. We were all in awe at this beautiful creature and I quietly chuckled to myself. It has been an honour to know Andrea and she's an excellent teacher. As she would say, "It's all about the journey. You are not alone."

Where would I be without my friends? Truly, they have been there for me in their own way and have seen me from my lowest to my highest points. Let me tell you about one of them. I met Anna through my psychic friend Lucy, and Anna is a firecracker. She is very spiritual, and I clicked with her as soon as I met her. Anna is just what you need because she too was involved with a narcissist, and she got out – so she just gets it. Anna lifted me up when I felt truly broken, and she has seen me blossom. I was at her house one day in 2020 and she took a picture of me, and I looked completely different. At last, I had fire in my eyes and soul. Nobody could dislike Anna. She is the kind of person who is sociable and authentic.

Then there is my friend Tamara, who I met whilst doing *The Artist's Way* many years ago, when I was married. She was such a support for me when I was going through my divorce. Tamara introduced me to new music and a great live music venue called Spiritual Bar, and it was just what my soul cried out for when I needed to get away from my husband. I love seeing her own unique spirituality unfolding. Those musical nights were also instrumental towards my healing.

My spiritual guides gave me so much strength throughout my

divorce, even when I couldn't see it at the time. They are able to give me strength and perspective to see the bigger picture. My brother Chris was the one who took me seriously when I was a young girl. He knew that I would write about my life. Chris was there in spirit when I attended a shamanic workshop at Atlantis Spiritual Centre in 2018. I saw a woman looking at me. She must have noticed my curiosity, as she came up to speak to me. As I looked back at her, I intuitively knew she could see someone with me. She explained that she saw a spirit with me, and that they were pleased I was at the workshop. I believe it was my brother Chris. He often sent little signs that he was around me – I would find white feathers in obscure places in my home, and I found comfort in that connection. Sometimes he gave me information, and my psychic friend Lucy also saw him. More contact came through the shaman who did my soul retrieval. She told me information about my brother that confirmed things I had felt and believed. I never feel alone now because I can always ask for assistance from the helping spirits around me.

'If you become a helper of hearts,
springs of wisdom will flow from your heart.'

Rumi

While being an Indigo has been a challenge, that is about to change for empaths. The world is now going through a collective spiritual awakening. The energies on the earth grid are being upgraded to a higher frequency. The downside is that all the dark energy has to come up to be cleansed and purged in order for the new energy to come through. This is being felt by many people on an unconscious level. This means that worldwide issues such as corruption and injustice in every society will need to be exposed and acknowledged. We need awakened energy healers now more than ever. It is our time to shine light into the darkness.

This process all relates back to shamanism. Healers are the ones who can see in the dark; a shaman allows the light to come through and heal. In addition, as an Indigo, my soul mission is to help heal those in need and make a positive difference. This was also highlighted for me when I explored shamanic journeying and discovered my power animal, the snake. There were many snakes on that journey and I explained to the shaman just what I saw in my visions. The practitioner concluded: "You managed to turn something harmful into medicine to heal yourself."

The new energy that is coming back to us is the divine feminine. We must get in touch with this energy in order to help Mother Earth recover from centuries of oppression and damage. The world is going through a complete transformation now and while this is happening there is discomfort; it will be extremely painful but ultimately it will be worth it in the end.

Conclusion

I hope you have enjoyed reading my story, because it has certainly been a journey of transformation for me. There is no doubt that I have been able to find spiritual meaning from my experiences. When life gives you challenging situations, it takes a lot to transmute events that are hidden in darkness in order to shine a light. A Jedi would say it is all about the balance of light and dark merging into one. Difficulties become a great teacher.

A shaman is someone who can see things that are hidden. I have had to confront my shadows and shine a light on childhood wounds, narcissism and domestic abuse. It wasn't easy; it was downright hard at times. However, I know that when you light a candle it gives other people the opportunity to shine their own light. *Walking Through Fire* is about rediscovering my own internal power, and the element of fire is also symbolic of wisdom and knowledge.

Shamanism allowed me to examine my divorce as I discovered my power animals, who allowed me to find a way towards my healing path. It is rather fitting that, as I came to the end of writing the book, I did a power animal retrieval and asked an important question: "What is the lesson in all of this?" An eagle made a timely appearance and the words I heard were "Surrender, forgive yourself and forgive others."

Those words seem so fitting as I had indeed let go of the past and all the difficult emotions while writing my book. Now I can see the higher perspective and gifts of my personal situation. The eagle is a bird that can soar high and is known to commune with the creator. The crow will peck at the eagle, who will ignore this behaviour and instead fly to higher altitudes. The eagle takes a higher perspective, and this is something I have learnt to do throughout this journey of writing my book. On the new Nigerian flag there is a red eagle. That feels like a homage to my Nigerian grandfather.

I was able to commune with my guides whilst exiting my abusive marriage. The power animals gave me strength when I felt like all hope was lost. Panther showed me what was possible and enabled me to overcome any doubts I felt; she gave me the courage to write *Walking Through Fire*.

The voice is the most powerful tool we have, and I wanted to highlight parental alienation, a complex and multi-layered by-product of post separation abuse that has affected me.

Amazingly, after writing my book I came across the fact that when a baby grows in a woman, the cells of the baby migrate into the mother's bloodstream and go back into the baby. This also happens when there is a miscarriage. These cells are known as foetal maternal micro-chimerism and they circulate between mother and child for 41 weeks. When a mother's heart is hurt, the foetal cells will immediately help to mend it. How amazing is that? This is why I believe that, as a mother, I will always have a bond with my children, whether they are near or far. I can only continue to have unconditional love for them and speak my truth from my heart.

I want to make changes to the family court system as parental alienation (coercive control) is a form of psychological abuse; a hidden mental health issue and a silent epidemic within domestic abuse. The other added layer of narcissism is that it is hard to diagnose, and the current DSM framework only sees how it affects the person and not those around them, like children and intimate partners. If you have someone who has narcissism and you are intimate with them and have children and try to leave them, it becomes even more problematic. This is why compassion is needed for those who are in narcissistic family units. I managed to get out for my own mental wellbeing, but others will be trapped, and children are caught in the middle. Hopefully the reader will see how difficult it is for women to leave abusive relationships when systems are unable to fully support them.

I highlighted my experience with economic abuse as being a major factor in not leaving my marriage sooner. This was one reason for writing the book – to highlight economic abuse – and I want to make changes by educating professionals, especially Cafcass, courts and police, as this is a hidden aspect of domestic abuse that can be ongoing during the relationship and post separation. This indeed should be a red flag and should come up as a risk of abuse.

Narcissists never change and will continue to manipulate – that is why it's challenging to co-parent with people like this. The co-parenting relationship becomes non-existent as the narcissist increases manipulation techniques over time. This is because once a victim gets away, the narcissist uses their own children as weapons, knowing this will cause upset to the other parent. Manipulators use DARVO: this stands for Deny, Attack, Reverse Victim and Offender. This term was coined by psychologist Jennifer Freyd: "The offender rapidly creates the impression that the abuser is the wronged one, while the victim or concerned observer is the offender ... The offender is on the offense and the person attempting to hold the offender accountable is put on the defense." Manipulators will never take accountability, and no one will ever say to them, "Why don't you stop?"

As a mother, I am learning to heal my heart, and level up my own healing journey. As an Indigo soul, I want to make so many changes, and writing this book is part of the change that I want to see. My spiritual awakening was painful but, ultimately, it's what saved me. I had to rebuild a different version of myself. You see, my soul heard the call and I was chosen. It's not an easy path, but I knew that before I came here. I'm sure you'll agree that what the world needs is healing, right here, right now.

~~~

If you would like to take some next steps, come join my community.

Contact me via my website and join my mailing list for upcoming workshops: indigo-flame.com
~~~

An Interview with J.J. Jenneson

Where in the world are you from?

I'm originally from North London, currently live in South London, but someday I really want to live by the sea.

What made you write *Walking Through Fire*?

Writing a book has been an ambition of mine for a long time. I've had short plays produced, and written poetry and short stories. For me, I knew that writing about my life was going to be the biggest challenge. However, my soul was calling me to write my memoir. I wanted to help women going through difficult circumstances to feel less alone. Just because you are given a set of circumstances, it doesn't have to define you. Writing about my life was transformative and became my superpower. I wanted to release the shame of being in a toxic marriage and give courage and inspiration to other people going through challenging circumstances.

How long did it take?

It took about five months to write – and to be honest, that was the easy part. At first, I thought that would be the hardest part but actually writing the book was straightforward. Editing was the most difficult part of the process as I'm dyslexic, and I had to overcome obstacles.

You said the editing was difficult, but was that the most difficult part of writing the book?

My book is really personal and difficult emotions were bubbling up from the past. I found it ironic as I was writing about my trauma and didn't anticipate having to face up to the feelings that were buried within my memories, so in a way, writing about the trauma actually allowed me to express myself fully rather than hold me back. I had to feel whatever emotions were coming up for me, and it became cathartic, and I was able to have compassion and patience whilst going through the editing process. I'm dyslexic, so that also presented challenges that I needed to overcome.

What did you learn about yourself by doing this?

For me, it was about releasing fear and not caring about what people would think of me. It was a big challenge that I had to face, whilst writing. I realised that I could have a hundred reasons for not doing it, but in the end, courage gave me the power to tell my story. I realised that it was going to be difficult emotionally and then I realised it only mattered what I think and how I interpreted those events in my life. I had to have trust and faith in the process of writing my truth. I was able to go beyond the challenge of being dyslexic and do something that I didn't think was possible. I had some other external issues in my personal life whilst writing my book. This proved to me that I'm extremely resilient.

When you're not writing, what are your hobbies?

I enjoy spending time at the seaside, hanging out with my friends, sitting under trees, watching movies, singing, dancing and listening to spiritual teachers, as I am constantly evolving in my own self-development.

Now that the book is finished, what's the next step for you?

I would love for people to learn about shamanism and I'm passionate about power animals, as I believe they are a great healing modality. Shamanism has transformed my life, and I would like to share it with as many people as possible. It's an amazing spiritual practice. I plan to run workshops on issues around trauma and economic abuse. There is so much work that needs to be done around domestic abuse and I want to advocate for women and educate professionals within the system. There are many changes that still need to be made. As a survivor of domestic abuse, I can see the gaps within services for women who have left abusive situations.

And what's the big dream for you?

I am fascinated by eco houses and would love to have a healing centre by the sea. I'm learning about the laws of the land. This is also known as natural law, universal law and common law and with this comes our inalienable right, which are given to us from birth by our creator. I love the link between shamanism and common law. This is also about the law of the land and the natural powers held within us. The whole world is evolving, and I look forward to a better world that is coming for everybody.

Do you think you might write another book?

I'll never say never. I have lots of ideas and I'm in the process of writing a play.

Oh wow, that's news. So, what will that be about?

I'm not sure yet. I may decide to make it partly autobiographical. I have been writing a screenplay and I want to incorporate shamanic themes with comedy. I have a dark sense of humour, so I'll need to see what I can do with that. There really are so many possibilities.

Lastly, just for me. What made you choose Butterfly House Publishing to help you write and publish your book?

I really enjoyed working with this company as it is very heart-centred. It's something that resonated with me, and there is a story about a butterfly in *Walking Through Fire*, which is symbolic as butterflies are symbols of resurrection, renewal, endurance and spiritual transformation.

Further Reading

One Mom's Battle: Divorcing a Narcissist – Tina Marie Swithin

Co-parenting with a Toxic Ex – Amy Baker

Why Does He Do That? – Lundy Bancroft

The Vein of Gold: A Journey to Your Creative Heart – Julia Cameron

~~~

If you would like to work with me: www.indigo-flame.com
~~~

Acknowledgements

Writing a list to say thank you is an interesting experience. I'd like to gratefully acknowledge and send my loving appreciation to the following people; I am so sorry if I have left anyone out. Thank you to:

My children: You are wonderful spiritual beings. I am so blessed, and I learn so much about life from you both. I am in awe that the creator believed in me to be your mum.

My sisters and family of origin: Thank you for your support during my divorce.

Lisa Jago: You are my soul sister; thank you for your love and support. I am blessed to have you in my life. Love and light to you always.

Andrea Lowry: Thank you for your creativity and for highlighting the importance of play through The Artist's Way group. You are a fantastic teacher.

Nick Constance: I know you wanted to be part of my story and I know you are still looking out for me. I am so grateful for your support.

Tamara C: Thank you for those nights at the spiritual bar listening to live music, and all our talks about *The Artist's Way* and spiritual stuff.

The Artist's Way Group: Thank you for your wonderful insight and support as we rediscovered our creativity.

Anna Chiodo: You are one of a kind and a kindred spirit. Thanks for being a lovely friend.

Lucy Mackonochie: I love your perspective. Thank you for all your insights with my brother Chris and your words of encouragement.

Romilly Golding: Thank you for your wonderful insights and feedback on my ideas and for providing invaluable clarity during the editing process of *Walking Through Fire*.

Sonia Braham: I'm so proud of you and all you have achieved with your work in domestic violence. Thanks for interviewing me and other women about our experiences and for taking your findings to the Houses of Parliament and speaking with Lady Hilary Armstrong.

Crow Tribe at Atlantis Spiritual Centre and Les Fuller: You are all wonderful souls.

Think Like a Tree group: I have so much gratitude for this group. I have learnt so much about trees and I will cherish those magical Saturday morning classes with Andrea. A special shout out goes to Bengy and Rahim for providing valuable feedback.

Ellen Watts: Wow, thank you for being on my support team, for your Zen-like approach and belief that I could do this. You have a great, heartfelt energy of loving support. It has been a pleasure working with **Butterfly House Publishing**. Yes, and thank you for helping to make it become my reality. Yay, I did it!

Alison Thompson: Thank you for doing a stellar job with editing, making sense of my story and getting it out to the world. You are indeed the magical Proof Fairy. I really appreciate your enthusiasm for my book.

Meena Julien: What an amazing experience it was to have professional photos taken. I had a great time and loved the process.

To my ex-husband: I have learnt so many lessons. Thank you for highlighting what I needed to change within myself; That you were a good teacher. I am beginning to see that my trials have a divine purpose.

MATCH is a charity that gives support and advice to mothers who are apart from their children through family separation or a variety of other reasons. Thank you, MATCH. You have been a wonderful support to me in my time of need, especially those other mums who understand how I feel.

Bibliography

Ingerman, Sandra – Shamanic Journeying: A Beginner's Guide

Frances, Paul – The Shamanic Journey (Volume 1 in the Therapeutic Shamanism series)

Frances, Paul – Rewilding Yourself (Volume 2 in the Therapeutic Shamanism series)

Thomas, ME – Confessions of a Sociopath

Morningstar, Dana – Out of the Fog: Moving from Confusion to Clarity After Narcissistic Abuse

Cameron, Julia – The Artist's Way: A Course in Discovering and Recovering your Creative Self

Levy, Paul – Dispelling Wetiko: Breaking the Curse of Evil

Printed in Great Britain
by Amazon

78151454R00092